Pascal's Manale Cookbook

Pascal's Manale Cookbook

A Family Tradition

Home of

THE ORIGINAL B-B-Q SHRIMP

Poppy Tooker

PELICAN PUBLISHING COMPANY

GRETNA 2018

(Photograph by Sam Hanna)

Contents

	Introduction	9
Chapter 1	The Family	13
Chapter 2	Oysters	53
Chapter 3	Appetizers	79
Chapter 4	Gumbos and Soups	91
Chapter 5	Sauces, Salads, and Sandwiches	109
Chapter 6	Seafood	137
Chapter 7	Meat	169
Chapter 8	Spaghetti and Sides	191
Chapter 9	Desserts	209
	Acknowledgments	222
	Index	223

(Photograph by Sam Hanna)

Introduction

There are many jewels in New Orleans' culinary crown: Antoine's, Arnaud's, and Galatoire's, to name a few. Often hidden amongst this lofty list is Pascal's Manale, a century-old, Uptown neighborhood gem that is New Orleans' second-oldest, continuously operating family-owned restaurant. Only Antoine's seniority exceeds Pascal's in that category, as their family tradition of hospitality dates back to 1840. There, the similarities end.

The seventy-three-year difference between the founding of the two restaurants tells the story of the evolution of the Crescent City's food scene. Antoine Alciatore came from France in the mid-nineteenth century and was a major player in the formation of French Creole food. Frank Manale arrived from Palermo, Sicily at the close of the nineteenth century. Frank and his family brought with them a radically different flavor palette and pantry of ingredients. Salty anchovies, rich, red tomato gravies, and slippery spaghetti were the favored fare of Sicilians.

Different from the chef-driven dishes of the French immigrants, Sicilian food came from Mama's kitchen. When Frank Manale opened his restaurant, his Sicilian mama, Mamie, and her sisters were part of the family operation from its earliest days. The Manale men—Frank, his brothers, and eventually his nephews—all worked at the restaurant and bar on Napoleon Avenue. But blocks away, first in the Broadmoor neighborhood and later in the Garden District, the women in the family worked as well. From those home kitchens came Manale's classic meatballs and red gravy, tufoli, and stuffed artichokes.

Again and again over the last century plus, Sicilian family tradition and honor kept Manale's flame burning. Through Prohibition and the Great Depression, through World Wars and the untimely deaths of family members, the restaurant always came first and New Orleans residents responded with a love and loyalty that carries on today.

My culinary exploration of the French Creoles began in 2012, when I updated the book *Mme. Bégué's Recipes of Old New Orleans Creole Cookery*. Next, I researched and wrote *Tujague's Cookbook*. Tujague's Restaurant is the second-oldest continuously operating restaurant in New Orleans. Having told the nineteenth-century story of Tujague's and Bégué's French Creole food, it seemed logical to turn my attention next to the Sicilian evolution of Creole food. There's no better way to taste and learn that tale than from Pascal's Manale's Sicilian-New Orleans family.

I have youthful memories of pepper-laced, butter-laden, barbeque shrimp there, and I have slurped many a cold, salty oyster at the bar, but that's where my familiarity with Manale's ended. Manale's chef, Mark DeFelice, and I were mere acquaintances when I began to pursue him about the importance of this chronicle—the story of his family's Sicilian-New Orleans heritage through their history and their food.

What a delicious treat it has been to delve into their rich history while getting to know the fourth generation and fifth generation who carry on their family's restaurant tradition. I'm grateful to Mark and his family for welcoming me in.

Pascal's Manale Cookbook

food

break

June

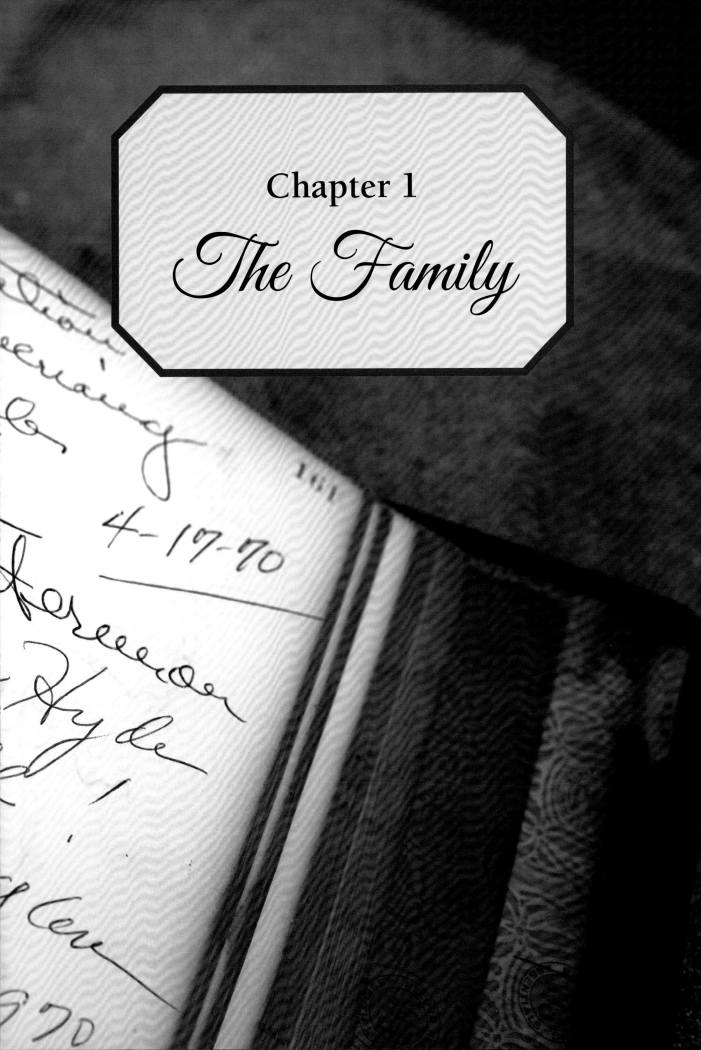

Chapter 1
The Family

Dressed in his best suit of clothes, twelve-year-old Frank Manale boarded the SS *Italia* on April 22, 1892, at the Palermo dock along with his parents, Francesco and Domenica (Mamie), and his six siblings, Francesca, Margherita, Antonina (Nene), Gioacchino (Jake), Rosalia (Lilly), and Paolo (Paul). Frank was the middle child in a family whose ages ranged from twenty to two years.

Packed aboard along with the immigrants were citrus fruits, figs, olives, and preserved tomatoes, not for the travelers' consumption but for the American market. On the return trip to Italy, the steamship would carry Louisiana-grown cotton and rice.

The voyage across the Atlantic lasted a month and the ship docked safely at the port of New Orleans on May 23, 1892. The New Orleans that welcomed the Manale family teemed with fellow Sicilians. Between 1880 and 1929, an estimated one hundred thousand people poured in through the port. Most Sicilians settled in the back of the French Quarter, an area that became known as "Little Palermo."

Forty-six-year-old Francesco listed his occupation as merchant, typical of the enterprising, hardworking Italian immigrants of the time. Hawking fruits and vegetables from handcarts in the streets, many eventually saved enough money to open small, corner groceries. Others purchased tracts of land on the Northshore of Lake Pontchartrain, where they farmed vegetables of all sorts and were especially noted for strawberry cultivation. Some rented stalls and others sold from trucks at the old French Market, which could have been called the Italian Market by the early 1900s.

It's important to note that the Manale family did not consider themselves to be Sicilian. Their town of origin was Contessa Entellina, an Albanian-founded city with its own dialect. The residents were referred to as Arbreshe and practiced a Byzantine form of Catholicism. Many distinguished New Orleans names derive from there—Monteleone, Tortorich, and Schiro, to name a few. Once in New Orleans, they lived as separately from the other Sicilians as they had in Sicily.

Founded in 1886, the Contessa Entellina Society is the oldest of the Italian social clubs in New Orleans and is still active today. These mutual aid and fraternal organizations were vital in assisting the assimilation of new immigrants. The society provided a doctor, a pharmacist, and a burial crypt. Even into the twenty-first century, only men who can prove their direct male lineage from Contessa Entellina are allowed membership.

Two years after arriving in New Orleans, Frank's sister Francesca married Matteo (Martin) Joseph Radosta, another immigrant from Contessa Entellina. Francesca and Martin had seven children together—Pascal, Lulu, Mamie, Frank, Vitda Rose, Peter, and Jake—who later became the backbone of what today is Pascal's Manale Restaurant.

(Photograph courtesy of The Historic New Orleans Collection)

Early family gathering (Photograph courtesy of DeFelice Family Collection)

Buchler Grocery, 1905 (Photograph courtesy of DeFelice Family Collection)

In 1913, Frank Manale rented a space previously occupied by the P. Buchler Grocery, located on the corner of Napoleon Avenue and Dryades Street, and opened a restaurant. In a practice common in those days, Dixie beer acquired exclusivity at Manale's by providing the Brunswick bar that still graces the restaurant today.

Next door to the restaurant was a butcher shop operated by Charles Ciaccio, who proved an excellent neighbor, providing Manale's with the freshest, best-quality meats. This arrangement continued until 1954, when the shop closed and Manale's expanded into the space with a large banquet room.

Frank Manale married Alice Hager in the 1920s. They had no children, but Alice had a daughter, Dolores, whom Frank raised as his own.

When asked about Frank Manale in a 2017 interview, Martin H. Radosta said, "He was a bootlegger who owned racehorses and loved to play the stock market before the 1929 crash." Manale's liquor sales proved profitable from the start, but even before Prohibition there were legal problems. In 1917, three years before Prohibition began, newspapers reported that Frank Manale and his nephew Pascal Radosta were arrested for allowing Albert Allamora, a sixteen-year-old delivery boy, to deliver alcohol.

Manale's issues with alcohol and the law predictably accelerated once Prohibition began on January 1, 1920. After all, in general, New Orleanians ignored the ban on alcohol as much as possible. When Izzy Einstein, a federal agent of the

Pascal and Pete Radosta at Manale bar pre-Prohibition (Photograph courtesy of DeFelice Family Collection)

(Photograph courtesy of DeFelice Family Collection)

Pete Radosta, Pascal Radosta, Sr., Frank Radosta, Sam Martina, Jake Radosta, Frank Manale
(Photograph courtesy of DeFelice Family Collection)

U.S. Prohibition Unit, arrived in the city, it took him only thirty-five seconds to make an arrest. Einstein hopped into a taxi at the train depot and asked where he could get a drink. The driver reached under his seat, produced a bottle, and was promptly handcuffed for his efforts. At Manale's—along with the advertised oyster loaves, club sandwiches, and Italian spaghetti—absinthe frappes and other alcoholic beverages were served secretly in coffee cups throughout the entire period of federally enforced temperance.

Once Prohibition ended, the party at Manale's continued. It was advertised in the *New Orleans Times-Picayune,* "Liquors are delivered promptly to homes day and night to all sections of the city." There was the added feature that "if you do not care to step out of the car and into the bar for your favorite cocktail or highball, drive by Manale's and you will be promptly served at the curb."

Aside from the butcher shop next door, there was a barbershop located in the rear of the building and a bookie on premises as well. Undoubtedly, much cash changed hands there, and despite Frank's claim that he never brought the day's receipts home with him, some thought otherwise.

In 1930, just before midnight one night, Frank and Alice drove up to the garage at their Elba Street home and were rushed by two gunmen, who shouted, "Now we got you! Stick 'em up!" Frank raised his left hand, reaching for his gun with his right.

Luckily, his nephew and namesake, Frank Radosta, lived just down the street.

(Photograph courtesy of DeFelice Family Collection)

He was also driving home from the restaurant and heard shots. Frank pursued the armed thieves to South Rendon Street, until one of the gunmen turned and fired point blank at him, at which point he wisely abandoned the chase. His uncle Frank was rushed to Baptist Hospital with a gunshot wound to the shoulder. There, he insisted to the police that there was no one who "wanted to get him." Nonetheless, it should be noted that firearms were common at Manale's. Initially, guns were hung on nails near the cash register. Later, they were kept discretely in small cubbyholes that are still there today.

Despite all his success, Frank Manale was not known for his smile. Few photos of him remain, but in each he maintains a serious demeanor, often surrounded by smiling family members. One family photo shows everyone relaxing on the porch in Mandeville, Louisiana, at a country house enjoyed by the family for generations.

In November of 1937, what Frank dismissed as a bad cold turned out to be double pneumonia. Less than forty-eight hours after taking ill, he died at home on November 29, at the age of fifty-seven. He was laid to rest in the family tomb in Greenwood Cemetery, leaving the restaurant in the capable hands of his Radosta nephews.

Pascal Radosta had been a fixture behind the Manale's bar since its earliest days. When his uncle opened the restaurant in 1913, Pascal was nineteen and one of the first employees. Written accounts proclaimed Pascal "one of the most capable and experienced bartenders in New Orleans," at "the same old Manale's, where for over twenty five years, many a businessman dropped in for a sociable drink with a friend."

A natural leader, Pascal quickly assumed the reins at Manale's, eventually calling the restaurant Pascal's Manale. His brothers, Pete, Jake, and Frank, stayed on after Frank Manale's death. Pete was a waiter, Jake cooked, and Frank tended bar, keeping the restaurant running smoothly.

Manale Mandeville camp—back row: Mamie Radosta, Florentine Radosta, Alice Ferran, Dolores Ferran, Alice Manale, Frank Manale; front row: Charles Ferran, Paul Manale (Photograph courtesy of Radosta Family Collection)

Manale's, late 1930s (Photograph courtesy of Radosta Family Collection)

Christmas 1938 (Photograph courtesy of Radosta Family Collection)

In 1939, Pascal Radosta hosted a testimonial dinner at Manale's honoring his brother Pete. In attendance that night—seated: Dr. Sam Houston (third from left), Bob Ainsworth (behind flowers), Pascal Radosta, Pete Radosta, Sam Saia; standing: Eva Talbot (holding drink), Charles Ciaccio, Ralph Alexis, Charlie Degan, Emile Zatarain, Johnny Brown, Francis Mora. (Photograph courtesy of DeFelice Family Collection)

In 1922, Pascal had married Frances Sansone, a devout Catholic who had been convent bound, before her parents persuaded her to marry the dashing Pascal. They settled on Louisiana Avenue Parkway in New Orleans' Broadmoor neighborhood, where they raised four children, Frances, Virginia, Pascal Jr. (always known as "Junior"), and Martin John.

In the kitchen there, Pascal's wife, Frances, and his sisters Lulu and Mamie cooked for the restaurant every day, stuffing artichokes and cooking meatballs with red gravy and other Manale favorites.

Not one of Pascal's three sisters ever married. For most of her life, however, Vitda Rose kept company with the championship boxer Pete Herman. Because Herman was a divorced man, Pascal forbade them to wed. They remained a devoted couple, however, frequently dining in a small, private room at Manale's.

The restaurant was a neighborhood hub, frequented by politicians, celebrities, sports figures, and locals alike. Everyone wanted to be a pal of Pascal, who was affectionately known as "Pas," including F. Edward Hebert, Louisiana's longest-serving member of the U.S. House of Representatives. After serving his first decade in Congress, Hebert gave credit to Pascal for his success, inscribing in the guestbook, "It all began at Manale's with Pascal."

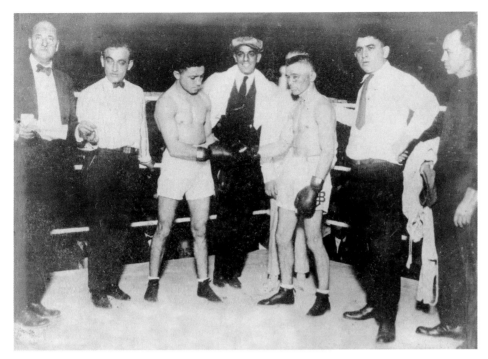

Boxing match—Pete Herman and Johnny Buff (Photograph courtesy of DeFelice Family Collection)

Pascal and F. Edward Hebert (Photograph courtesy of DeFelice Family Collection)

F. Edward Hebert and Committee on Naval Affairs, March 9, 1941 (Photograph courtesy of DeFelice Family Collection)

Committee on Naval Affairs, March 9, 1941 (Photograph courtesy of DeFelice Family Collection)

Pascal Radosta, Pascal Radosta, Jr., Jake Radosta, F. Edward Hebert, during World War II
(Photograph courtesy of DeFelice Family Collection)

At the restaurant, Pascal—not the customer—was always right. Hebert observed, "Manale's is the only restaurant I know where the customer is always wrong. I would come in and order steak and he [Pascal] would say, 'You're not going to get steak; you're going to get oysters.' And so I ate oysters. He ran the restaurant as he pleased. If a customer whose look he didn't like walked through the doors, with the bar packed with patrons, he would tell him, 'I'm sorry but we're closed.'"

The restaurant closed on Tuesdays, which became family night on Louisiana Avenue Parkway. Dinner at Pascal's home was a highly sought after invitation. Food was sent over from the restaurant, and a festive evening was guaranteed. Pascal was a great opera lover and he passed that love on to his children, who entertained the guests after dinner. Virginia would play piano, and both Frances and Martin John would sing.

Although Frances's ability to hold a tune is the subject of debate, Pascal fostered her love of opera with voice lessons. Pascal was also a great supporter of the New Orleans Opera Association. Playbills from the 1940s and '50s list both Frances and her brother Martin John as members of the ensemble. Later in life, Frances remained an active member of the Opera Association, often hosting gala fundraisers at Manale's.

But it wasn't just Frances who liked to sing! In the 1950s, Manale's bar was

Pascal, Virginia, and Pascal Radosta, Jr. (Photograph courtesy of DeFelice Family Collection)

a favorite nightspot of an off-duty policeman, who after a drink or two would begin to belt out selections from popular operas of the day. During one such performance, in a fit of heightened passion, the officer drew his gun in the crowded bar, accidentally firing it. Mortified, the policeman fled, but the bullet remains lodged in the back bar today.

After Pascal's brother Frank died in 1942, Frank's son, Martin Henry Radosta, often stayed at his uncle's home. In the Radosta family, it was a tradition to name the first grandson after his grandfather. When Pascal named his first son Pascal—instead of honoring "Papa"—his father, Matteo (Martin) Radosta, never quite got over the slight. Perhaps because of the commotion his elder brother caused, Frank

Virginia Radosta (Photograph courtesy of DeFelice Family Collection)

(Photograph by Sam Hanna)

named *his* firstborn Martin, when he was born in 1932. Consequently, the birth of Pascal's youngest, who was named Martin *John*, created an abundance of Martins in one house!

Martin H. remembered those days on Louisiana Avenue Parkway very well. Every morning, Papa and Uncle Jake would wake him for the trip down to the French Market to purchase fresh produce and seafood for the restaurant. Early on, Martin became one of Manale's delivery boys. One of his favorite jobs was picking up meatballs and gravy from his aunt Frances, Pascal's wife, before heading over to Leidenheimer's Bakery for the day's French bread. An added benefit to the job was dunking the hot bread into the gravy for a quick treat before making the delivery to the restaurant.

Everyone in the family worked at the restaurant, even the family pet! Junior had a German shepherd named Bruno who guarded the restaurant at night. When the doors were locked, Bruno was set loose inside to prevent any would-be robbers from attempting to break in.

Martin Henry and Martin John Radosta
(Photograph courtesy of Radosta Family Collection)

Pascal, Pete, Jake, Martin John, Pascal, Jr. (Photograph courtesy of DeFelice Family Collection)

Pascal, Jr., Bruno, Martin (Papa) Radosta (Photograph courtesy of DeFelice Family Collection)

Actually, the female family members didn't work at Pascal's Manale. Pascal's wife, Frances, and sisters were kept busy cooking at home on Louisiana Avenue Parkway. His daughters, Frances and Virginia, led the lives of young socialites.

When not musically engaged, Frances and Virginia were seen at Mardi Gras balls and other parties around town. Fittingly, the Radosta sisters were great friends of restaurateur Owen Brennan's daughters, Ella and Adelaide. Hotelier Frank Monteleone's daughter, Isabel, also ran with their crowd.

In 1954, Vincent Sutro, a racing fan and great friend of Pascal's, told his friend about an unusual shrimp dish he'd recently enjoyed in Chicago. Pascal and his brother Jake went into the kitchen together and soon presented Sutro with a version of the dish they'd improvised. Sutro proclaimed their version to be even better than what he remembered. They called it barbeque shrimp, because of its bright-red color and peppery sauce. It was such a hit that soon, Pascal added it to the Manale menu, changing the course of New Orleans' culinary history forever.

Paul Piazza, Jr., seafood dealer, 1950s (Photograph courtesy of DeFelice Family Collection)

Pascal in an apron, ready to cook some barbeque shrimp! (Photograph courtesy of DeFelice Family Collection)

From the early 1950s, every celebrity, sports star, and politician who came through the restaurant's doors signed the cordovan leather-bound guestbook. Throughout the pages of the book, there are memorable remarks from an amazing array of people. Here's a sampling.

Marilyn Monroe and escort, Gregory Peck
December 10, 1959

"A great lunch—Best Wishes"
Arnold Palmer—October 6, 1959

"Best dinner this side of the moon"
Buzz Aldrin—January 10, 1970

"For Pascal's, Thanks for an Excellent BBQ Shrimp dinner"
Julius "Dr. J" Erving

"Sloppy shrimp—got on my shirt—Good though—"
Elton John, London, England

Often, autographed photos were sent in thanks for the delicious memories Manale's made for famous visitors during their New Orleans visit, a tradition that began in the 1940s and continues today. In no particular order, the photos skip through decades of notables. George Burns, Bette Midler, ZZ Top, and Liberace all share space on the walls of Manale's bar.

(Photograph by Sam Hanna)

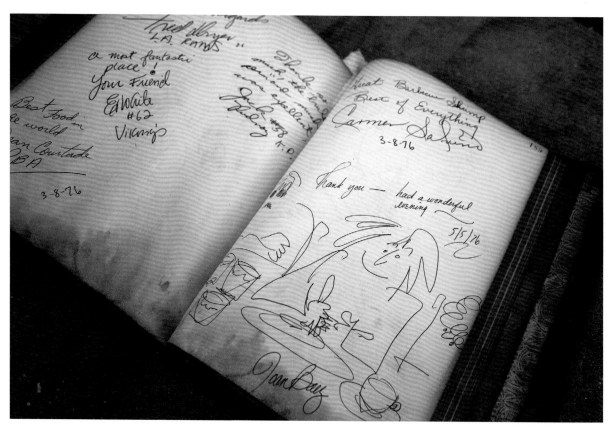

(Photograph by Sam Hanna)

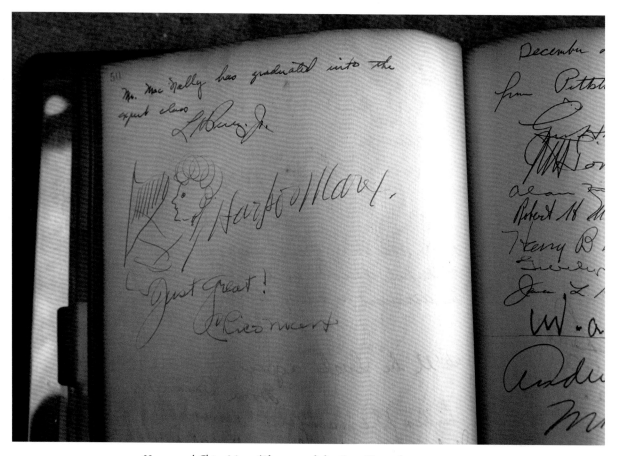

Harpo and Chico Marx (Photograph by Sam Hanna)

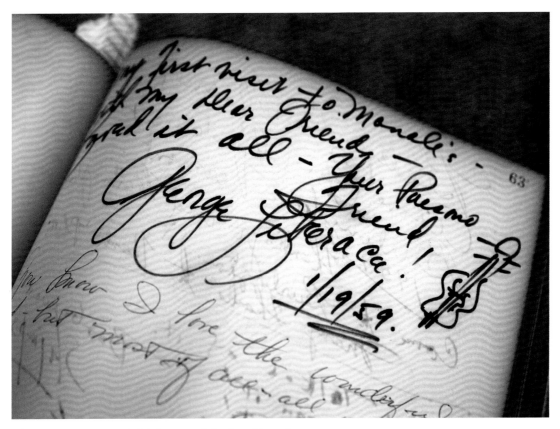

Liberace, January 19, 1959 (Photograph by Sam Hanna)

(Photograph courtesy of DeFelice Family Collection)

Pascal was so beloved by his friends that on May 17, 1954, they threw a party for him at his own restaurant, an unusual occurrence to say the least. All of New Orleans' greatest names in business, law, and medicine were in attendance, savoring hot boiled crawfish and cold steins of beer.

Pascal's grandson Esteff (Bob) DeFelice was just five years old when his grandfather died, but he has vivid memories of spending time at Manale's with him. Sitting right up at the bar, he'd be served his favorite drink—a Roy Rogers with extra cherries—which he remembers once sipping in the company of singer

Pascal's party, May 17, 1954—seated in center: Eva Talbot, F. Edward Hebert, Pascal Radosta; standing: Bill Coker, Frank Von Der Haar (Photograph courtesy of DeFelice Family Collection)

Pascal's party, May 17, 1954 (Photograph courtesy of DeFelice Family Collection)

Frankie Laine. But most of all, Bob loved the Dubble Bubble bubblegum that Pascal always had available in his office for the grandchildren.

The pinball machine in the bar was a particular source of fascination for Pascal's grandson Sandy DeFelice. He loved watching the bar's patrons play the twenty-five-hole machine as the steel balls careened about, sometimes hitting it big. The Manale's pinball machine actually paid winnings: a nickel for each credit. Often, a patron would cash in 400 credits for a twenty-dollar bill—not small change in those days!

Once Sandy told his grandfather that he wished he could have a pinball like the ones in the machine. The next time he visited the restaurant, Pascal smiled and said, "Sandy, I've got something for you!" Pascal reached into his suit pocket and handed his grandson two steel pinballs—something Sandy has never quite forgotten.

In the early evening of July 23, 1958, Pascal was in his office at the restaurant watching a boxing match televised from Houston, Texas. As the match between Joe Brown and Kenny Lane progressed, Pascal suddenly suffered a heart attack. He collapsed and died in the bar, near the pinball machine. Once again, the tightly knit family came together to keep Pascal's spirit alive in the restaurant he had so loved. Junior and his brother, Martin John, worked closely with their uncles, Pete and Jake, maintaining the Manale's tradition.

Pascal's daughters, Frances and Virginia, married brothers, Stephen and Savare DeFelice, who hailed from Myrtle Grove, Louisiana, in Plaquemines Parish. The brothers operated a canning factory there, right on the water. The factory operated year round, canning whatever was in season. Oyster and shrimp fishermen pulled

Pascal III (Jay), Junior, Martin Henry, Jake, Martin John, August 24, 1968 (Photograph courtesy of Radosta Family Collection)

right up to the dock, unloading their freshly caught wares. Figs, tomatoes, and other produce that grew abundantly along the alluvial banks of the Mississippi River were also canned for sale.

While Frances and Steve were childless and remained in New Orleans, Virginia and her husband, Savare, chose the country life for their children, but Manale's truly remained their home away from home. As each addition to the growing family arrived, Virginia and Savare would bring the new baby straight to the restaurant from Touro Hospital before heading home to Myrtle Grove.

Mark DeFelice recalls his childhood in Myrtle Grove as particularly idyllic. The DeFelice children had their own pirogues, small boats that were easy to navigate in the calm, shallow waters surrounding their home. They hunted and fished, spending most of their days outdoors.

DeFelice's Delight label (Photograph courtesy of DeFelice Family Collection)

Myrtle Grove Packing Company (Photograph courtesy of DeFelice Family Collection)

The little boys from the bayou enjoyed their own form of sledding. There was a mountain of oyster shells next to the packing plant, a result of years of shucking oysters for canning. The enterprising crew found a length of corrugated metal, which they used like a sled to careen down the three-story-high hill of shells.

Eventually, Virginia and Savare moved the family closer to New Orleans. The original DeFelice home was cut into three pieces and physically moved to Belle Chasse on trucks. Ginny was at recess in second grade and remembers seeing the house go by from the playground.

As time marched on, Junior and Martin John retired, leaving Manale's in Frances's and Virginia's care. For Frances, Manale's was an extension of the glamorous life she'd always sought. With her glittering, diamond shrimp brooch pinned to her shoulder and gold, diamond-tipped swizzle stick dangling around her neck, Frances appeared as much of a VIP as the celebrities who frequented the restaurant. It was well known that no trip to New Orleans was complete without a meal at Manale's.

Throughout the 1960s and '70s, Manale's popularity was undiminished. Much of the time, Martin H. Radosta functioned as maître d', a job he relished. Most nights, the bar was packed with hungry guests waiting to be called for an open table. Martin would occasionally amuse himself by calling out over the loudspeaker, "Paging . . . " The din of the bar instantly quieted as people listened hopefully

Virginia, Savare, and children—back row: Sandy, Bob, Mark; front row: Ginny and Mary Frances (d. 1977), December 1963. (Photograph courtesy of DeFelice Family Collection)

Frances and Virginia (Photograph courtesy of DeFelice Family Collection)

Frances and Virginia arriving for a birthday celebration, April 1, 1985 (Photograph courtesy of DeFelice Family Collection)

Martin H. Radosta (Photograph courtesy of DeFelice Family Collection)

Bob, Sandy, Ginny, Savare, Virginia, and Mark, New Year's Eve 1988 (Photograph courtesy of DeFelice Family Collection)

for their name, giving Martin quite a chuckle. Some nights, the crowd was so thick that guests with reservations couldn't get to the podium and would call the restaurant from the payphone at the door, proclaiming, "We're here!"

And once you were there, Martin was not going to let you go! When told that there was a wait of an hour and a half, a regular customer protested, "Well, I'm not going to stay then." Martin grabbed a hammer, leaned over the bar, and said, "Come here." With that, he nailed the man's tie to the podium. Amazingly, the gentleman stayed put until his table was called. Martin released him from the bar, and he went quietly into the dining room for dinner.

Frances's nephews Jay (Pascal III) and Scott worked closely with her, assisting with the day-to-day management of the restaurant. After the death of her husband, Steve, in the 1980s, running the family business proved too much for Frances. Virginia and Savare became the sole proprietors, and the restaurant prospered under their careful guidance. Savare worked the front of the restaurant, and Virginia ran the office.

In keeping with the family tradition, Virginia and Savare's children, Sandy, Bob, Mark, and Ginny, worked various jobs at the restaurant throughout high school and college. Sandy and Bob held front-of-the-house positions, working as bartender

Manale's staff, early 1980s (Photograph courtesy of DeFelice Family Collection)

and maître d', while Mark gravitated toward the kitchen from the very start. Ginny occasionally worked as hostess but was most often found in the office, working alongside her mother.

Christmas and New Year's have always been great celebrations at Manale's. Ads from as early as 1924 invite guests to enjoy "wonderful Italian spaghetti" for Christmas Eve supper there. During Virginia and Savare's time, the entire DeFelice clan would gather at the family home in Myrtle Grove every Christmas Eve. New Year's Eve was always a big night for the family at Manale's.

One of the restaurant's greatest assets has always been the devoted staff, both in front and back of the house. Beloved waitress Catherine Daniels worked at Manale's for fifty years. Often requested by regulars, Catherine knew how to make everyone feel at home. Today, longtime waitress Wendy Gruntz continues the Manale's tradition of warm, personal hospitality.

Waitresses were always the norm at Manale's, but Pascal's brother Pete was the exception. Pete's domain was the dining room, where he attended to favorite customers for decades. It would be three generations before there was a waiter in the dining room again, but when Savare's eldest grandson, Tré DeFelice, expressed an interest in becoming a waiter, his grandfather acquiesced. Today, the service staff is an even mix of ladies and gentlemen.

New Year's Eve 1964 (Photograph by Dr. Lyon K. Loomis, courtesy of DeFelice Family Collection)

Nick Locicero, Virginia DeFelice, and "Seafood Sal" Navarra (Photograph courtesy of DeFelice Family Collection)

In 2016, the Louisiana Restaurant Association named Wendy Gruntz, along with Karry Byrd, Beverly Simon, Jessie Mae Felix, Vivian Spraul, and Thomas Stewart, Restaurant Legends for their many years of service.

Pascal's nephew Johnny Sansone was a fixture at Manale's bar for over fifty years. Johnny knew virtually everyone who came through the door and was always ready with great stories to tell. His favorite topic was sports, and Johnny could be counted on for the lowdown on the horses running at the track.

Nick Locicero and Johnny Bonano manned the oyster bar for decades, presenting guests with the icy-cold, salty Gulf oysters that Manale's has always been famous for.

"Uncle Jake," Pascal's youngest brother, spent most of his life at the restaurant. He was kitchen manager when Mark DeFelice, today's executive chef, came to work there. It was Uncle Jake who taught Mark to make his legendary cheesecake, often the first task he was given each morning. Jake passed on to Mark the family secrets of tufoli and lasagna, dishes prepared exactly as they had been by generations of Manale and Radosta family members before him.

(Photograph by Sam Hanna)

Frank Robinson, Fats Domino, Mark DeFelice (Photograph courtesy of DeFelice Family Collection)

Kenny and Karry Byrd, Virginia DeFelice, Luther and Thomas Stewart (Photograph courtesy of DeFelice Family Collection)

DeFelice family and Manale's staff, November 1990 (Photograph courtesy of DeFelice Family Collection)

Standing: Savare, Frances, Tré, Ginny, David DeFelice, and Virginia DeFelice, A. J. and Lydia Norman, Arleen and Sandy DeFelice; seated: Bob, Elizabeth, Dana, and Mark DeFelice, Mother's Day 1993 (Photograph courtesy of DeFelice Family Collection)

Standing: Dana, Tré, Kate, Kelly, Sandy, Arleen, Cathy, Bob, Elizabeth, Thomas, Mark, Esteff DeFelice; seated: Martin H. Radosta, Ginny, Brooks, Marci, Rachel, Pascal, David DeFelice (Photograph by Sam Hanna)

Frank Robinson worked as Manale's chef for many years. Before that, he had spent over twenty years at Brennan's restaurant on Royal Street. Frank passed his knowledge on to many of today's kitchen crew, who themselves have amazing longevity in their positions. Frank loved the music of Fats Domino and could be heard in the kitchen daily belting out his version of "Blueberry Hill."

Karry Byrd has worked in the Manale's kitchen for over forty years. At one time, his twin brother, Kenny, worked there as well. The Byrd family had long ties to the DeFelices through Karry and Kenny's mother, Camille, who worked for many years as Frances's housekeeper on Sixth Street. While still in school, Karry and Kenny did yardwork for Frances. Once they were old enough, there were jobs waiting for them at Manale's.

Karry began as a dishwasher and worked his way up to lead line cook. Today, he is responsible for most of the Manale standards, maintaining a culinary continuity that stretches back more than a century.

Beverly Simon is another piece of the valuable institutional memory of Manale's. "Miss Bev," as she is known, can do almost anything in the kitchen. She keeps the busy line moving along, handling a full load of orders at one time. Bev is also responsible for whipping up Pascal's Spicy Mayonnaise, an integral ingredient in many of the cold dishes and salads, including their renowned remoulade sauce.

Virginia and Savare's eight grandchildren relished the time they spent at the restaurant. David DeFelice, Sandy's son, recalls that every child's first job there consisted of dusting picture frames. The bar's walls are covered from floor to ceiling with framed family photos and autographed images of celebrities who have dined there, so they never ran out of work.

Rachel, Mark's daughter, would be positioned on a barstool under the watchful, doting eyes of the kitchen staff as she peeled shrimp. Although Marci, Rachel's sister, also grew up in the restaurant, she pursued a career in marketing in Washington, D.C., and her cousin Tré became a dentist.

After getting their first taste of kitchen life in the family restaurant, Rachel and David both pursued culinary careers. Esteff, Bob's eldest son, did as well, but now he gives restaurant patrons a taste of New Orleans hospitality in San Diego, where he resides.

Elizabeth, Ginny's daughter, loved to get her tiny hands into the bread pudding as a child, squishing stale French bread into eggs and milk. Today, Elizabeth is in charge of the restaurant's social media and books special parties, working alongside her mother in the office.

When Sandy isn't greeting guests at Manale's, his daughter Dana is often on duty at the podium. Bob's son Thomas is typical of the fifth generation. Thomas recalls working as a dishwasher, pantry prep, line cook, bar porter, bartender, busboy, waiter, and maître d' at the restaurant. One thing is certain. If there's a job to be done at Manale's, there's always a family member on duty to do it.

food

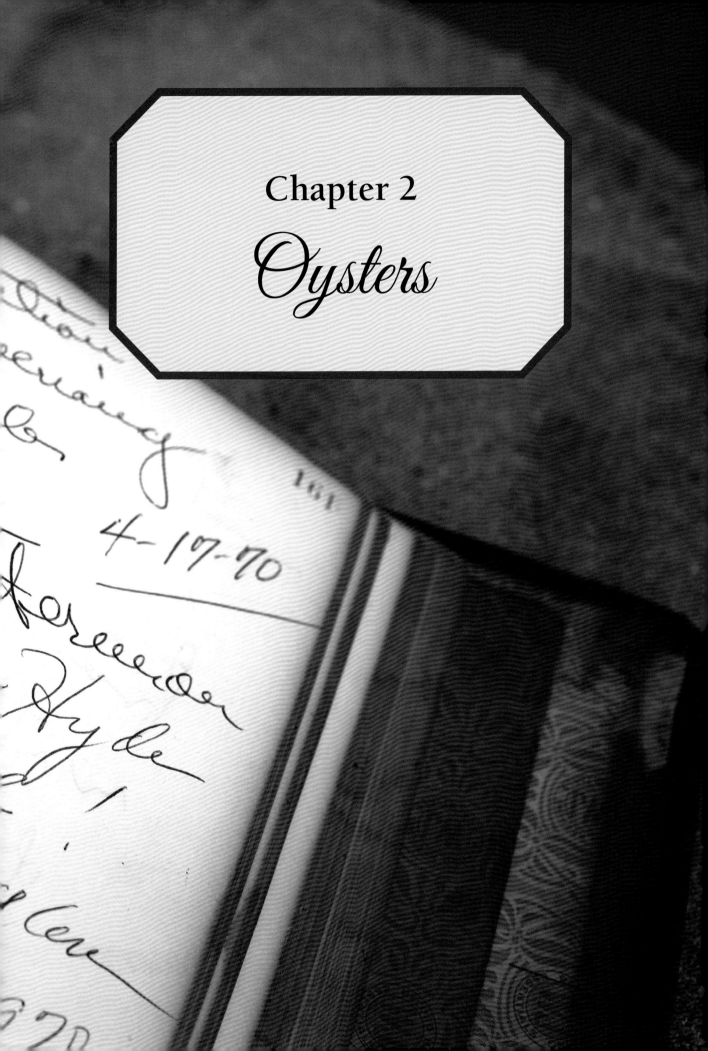

Chapter 2
Oysters

The century-old oyster bar, a bar within the Manale's bar, has been a fixture there since the establishment's earliest days. A 1925 ad promoted oysters by the dozen for just twenty cents!

An oyster bar is only as good as its shucker. Many a popular shucker has worked there, including Nick Locicero, whom the *Minneapolis Star* newspaper on July 11, 1979, described as a "74 year old white haired Italian and New Orleans native who presided over Manale's oyster bar for at least 20 years," along with his compatriot, Johnny Bonano, who claimed to regularly shuck over five thousand oysters a day.

Located to the right of the front door, inside the bar itself, Manale's oyster bar has always been one of its main attractions. Today, Thomas Stewart, better known as "Uptown T," holds court there most days. Thomas's career at Manale's began in December of 1979, when he first worked as a dishwasher. But he aspired to move up the kitchen ranks. When Thomas shared those ambitions with the chef, he was handed a knife and instructed to julienne vegetables for shrimp creole. Soon after, he began working as a prep cook and then became the salad man.

Thomas proved himself so invaluable in the kitchen that he had a bit of trouble making the transition to oyster shucker. In 1990, he saw the position advertised and asked Chef Mark DeFelice to consider him for the job. Although that's his primary role at the restaurant today, the kitchen still relies on his cooking skills for preparing Monday's traditional red beans and rice.

Pascal Radosta (left) and F. Edward Hebert (second from left) at the oyster bar (Photograph courtesy of DeFelice Family Collection)

"Uptown T," Thomas Stewart (Photograph by Sam Hanna)

How to Shuck Oysters

In the seventeenth century, author Jonathan Swift wrote, "He was a bold man that first ate an oyster." When Frank Manale opened his restaurant and bar in 1913, oystermen fished the beds from small boats designed by early French settlers they had dubbed *canots*. The wooden vessels' rounded bottoms and small fins allowed for easy passage through shallow waters. Eventually, the boats became known as "New Orleans oyster luggers." Oystermen harvested oysters using heavy, long-handled, scissor-like tongs with a rake on the bottom, and it was wet, backbreaking work.

When it comes to eating oysters, the first hurdle to overcome is shucking. Most South Louisiana oysters are grown on the muddy bottoms of our brackish estuaries. Sacks of oysters can be a messy, muddy affair, so first, the shells require a thorough hosing to remove as much dirt as possible. Every shell must be tapped to ensure it remains tightly closed, indicating the oyster inside is alive.

Oyster shucking can also be hazardous, so it's important to set up the shucking station using the right precautions. The hand that holds the oyster should be protected with a heavy glove. An oyster knife, with a short sharp blade, is a necessity, as are towels and a bowl for catching every drop of oyster liquor that runs out as the oysters are shucked. Nothing enhances an oyster dish more than that precious liquor, so save every drop. Any surplus can be frozen successfully for up to six months.

To open the oyster, insert the knife tip into the "hinge" at the back of the shell, wriggling around until you begin to feel a small gap form. When you find the muscle that keeps a live oyster tightly shut, twist the blade firmly to loosen it, then pry open the shell by running the knife blade around the edge, gently twisting the blade to separate the two halves.

When the halves are separated, discard the top shell, and fully detach the oyster from the muscle fiber that attaches it to the shell. This is the most important part of properly preparing an oyster to be eaten on the half-shell. Without the oyster being fully detached, the eater faces a struggle with the cocktail fork—not a pleasant experience, and something that would never happen at Manale's oyster bar!

(Photographs by Sam Hanna)

Oysters Bienville

Yields 2 dozen oysters

Virtually every old New Orleans restaurant lays claim to having invented Oysters Bienville. "Count" Arnaud Cazenave bolstered his by insisting that the dish was named for the street on which Arnaud's is located. Emile Commander, founder of another Uptown New Orleans classic restaurant, Commander's Palace, also asserted ownership. More plausible is Antoine's claim that the baked oyster dish dates back to the days of proprietor Roy Alciatore and Chef August Michel and was named for the city's founder, Jean-Baptiste Le Moyne, Sieur de Bienville. No matter the origin of the classic, Manale's secret flavor bomb of pureed bacon sets their version apart from the rest.

8 tbsp. butter
½ cup finely chopped onion
4 tbsp. finely chopped green bell pepper
¼ cup finely chopped celery
4 green onions, finely chopped
1 garlic clove, finely chopped
½ tsp. thyme
1 cup flour
1 cup light cream
½ cup sherry
6 slices bacon, chopped to a puree
½ cup finely chopped mushrooms
¼ lb. raw shrimp, peeled and finely chopped
1 tsp. salt
¼ tsp. white pepper
¼ tsp. cayenne pepper
4 tbsp. chopped fresh parsley
3 egg yolks
2 dozen oysters, poached
2 dozen oyster shells

Melt butter over medium heat in a saucepan. Add onion, bell pepper, celery, green onions, garlic, and thyme. Cook for 7-8 minutes.

Gradually stir in flour with a whisk, mixing until smooth. Cook for 5 minutes, stirring constantly until golden. Reduce heat to low and add the cream, whisking until smooth. When the sauce thickens, whisk in the sherry.

In a skillet, cook bacon until it begins to brown. Add mushrooms and shrimp and cook for 5 minutes, until mushrooms begin to brown and shrimp are pink. Sprinkle with salt and peppers, and stir in the parsley. Combine the bacon mixture with sauce.

In a double boiler, or over very low heat, beat egg yolks continuously until thickened. Add to the sauce, then remove from heat and cool. Fit a pastry bag with a fluted tip and fill the bag with the cooled sauce.

Place 1 poached oyster on each shell. Swirl Bienville Sauce on top of each oyster. Bake in a preheated 375-degree oven until lightly browned (about 20 minutes).

(Photographs by Sam Hanna)

(Photographs by Sam Hanna)

Oysters Rockefeller

Yields 2 dozen oysters

Oysters Rockefeller was invented by Jules Alciatore at his French Quarter restaurant, Antoine's, in 1899. They have never revealed their recipe, always asserting that despite the sauce's green color, spinach was not part of the dish. The Pascal's Manale version also lacks spinach, but it lives up to the name by being "as rich as Rockefeller."

3 stalks celery
1 bunch green onions
2 cups fresh parsley leaves
½ lb. butter, melted
¼ cup Lea & Perrins Worcestershire sauce
2 tbsp. hot sauce
½ cup Herbsaint or Pernod
1 cup Manale's Seasoned Breadcrumbs (see index)
2 dozen oysters, poached
2 dozen oyster shells

Combine celery, green onions, and parsley in food processor. Process until pureed. With the machine running, add the melted butter, Worcestershire, hot sauce, and Herbsaint.

Cook together in a saucepan for 5 minutes, until raw alcohol is cooked out. Stir in breadcrumbs to thicken, then cool. Fit a pastry bag with a fluted tip and fill the bag with the cooled sauce.

Put 1 poached oyster on each shell. Swirl Rockefeller Sauce on top of each oyster. Bake in a preheated 375-degree oven until lightly browned (about 20 minutes).

Oyster Stew

Serves 4

This stew, comprised of barely five ingredients, is the picture of delicious simplicity. Nothing is better on a chilly Louisiana day, when the oysters are at their salty best.

2 tbsp. butter
6 green onions, sliced
24 shucked oysters with oyster water
6 cups milk
White pepper to taste
1 tbsp. chopped fresh parsley
Salt and hot sauce to taste

Melt 1 tbsp. butter in a medium saucepan. Add green onions and sauté for 30 seconds. Add oyster water, milk, white pepper, and parsley.

Bring to a boil, then reduce to a simmer. Simmer for 5 minutes, then add oysters. Do not return stew to a boil.

Simmer gently for 2-3 minutes until oysters begin to curl and are poached. Season with salt and hot sauce. Serve with a small pat of butter on top of the stew.

Oyster Soup

Serves 6-8

Don't even attempt this dish without having the freshest oysters and, most importantly, that liquid gold known as "oyster water." This simple preparation allows the taste of the oyster to shine through.

¼ cup butter
¼ cup flour
1 onion, chopped
3 garlic cloves, chopped
6 green onions, finely chopped
2 stalks celery, chopped
¼ tsp. thyme
1 bay leaf
2 cups oyster water plus 1 cup water
2 dozen oysters (about 1 qt.)
½ tsp. chopped fresh parsley
Salt and pepper to taste

Melt the butter, then whisk in the flour, cooking over medium-high heat until light brown. Add onions and sauté for 10 minutes. Add garlic, green onions, and celery. Sauté all vegetables together for 15 minutes.

Add the thyme and bay leaf and sauté for an additional 5 minutes. Whisk in liquids and bring to a boil. Reduce to a simmer and add oysters, simmering until the oysters just begin to curl at the edges. Add parsley and season to taste with salt and pepper.

(Photograph by Sam Hanna)

Oyster and Artichoke Soup

Serves 6-8

Oyster and Artichoke Soup became a New Orleans menu staple after Chef Warren Leruth popularized it at his Gretna restaurant in the 1970s.

1 cup butter
1 medium onion, finely chopped
3 stalks celery, finely chopped
2 tsp. finely chopped garlic
1 cup flour
1 bay leaf
¼ tsp. thyme
½ gal. oyster water
2 8-oz. cans quartered artichoke hearts, drained
4 oz. heavy cream
1 qt. oysters, washed
¼ cup chopped green onions
¼ cup chopped parsley
¼ tsp. hot sauce
¼ tsp. white pepper
½ tsp. salt
½ tsp. Lea & Perrins Worcestershire sauce

Melt butter in a heavy saucepan. Add onions, celery, and garlic and sauté for 15 minutes. Whisk in flour and let cook for about 12-15 minutes.

Add bay leaf and thyme. Whisk in oyster water and bring to a boil. Reduce heat and simmer for 40 minutes.

Add artichokes. Simmer for 10 minutes. Add cream. Simmer for 10 minutes.

Add oysters, green onions, and parsley. Return to a simmer and add hot sauce, white pepper, salt, and Worcestershire.

How to Fry Oysters

Heat vegetable oil to 365 degrees. Oysters can be deep fried or pan fried.

To deep fry, add 3-4 inches oil to a saucepan deep enough to allow 3-4 additional inches above the level of the oil.

To pan fry, add ½ inch oil to a skillet.

Toss each raw oyster in cornmeal or corn flour. (This is a personal choice. Some people prefer the extra crunch that comes from coarse cornmeal, but Manale's uses corn flour seasoned with salt and pepper.)

Drop the oysters into the hot oil, being careful not to overcrowd the pan. (You don't want your oysters touching as they fry.) Fry for 2-3 minutes until lightly browned. Drain well and serve immediately.

(Photographs by Sam Hanna)

Oysters En Brochette Manale Style

Serves 4

Oysters wrapped in bacon were commonly known as "Angels on Horseback" in late-nineteenth-century Europe. In New Orleans, they acquired the name "Oysters En Brochette" and were typically served with a buttery meuniere sauce. In a nod to the family's Italian roots, Manale's Oysters En Brochette are wrapped in prosciutto before being fried to crisp perfection.

24 raw oysters
24 slices prosciutto, about 5 inches long
4 metal or bamboo skewers
2 cups flour
½ tsp. salt
½ tsp. pepper
1 egg
1 cup milk
1 tsp. hot sauce
Vegetable oil for deep frying

Wrap each oyster in 1 slice prosciutto. Skewer 6 wrapped oysters together. Season flour with salt and pepper. Beat egg together with milk and hot sauce.

Dip each skewer in flour, egg wash, then flour again. Fry in oil at 360 degrees for 3-4 minutes until lightly browned. Drain on a paper towel and serve.

Fried Oyster Spinach Salad with Warm Blue Cheese Dressing

Serves 4

Fried oysters and blue cheese make a perfect marriage in this stellar version of a spinach salad.

8 slices bacon, crisply cooked and crumbled
1 lb. fresh spinach
1 lb. white mushrooms, sliced
2 hardboiled eggs, sliced
12 fried oysters
1 cup Warm Blue Cheese Dressing (recipe follows)

Toss half of the bacon with spinach, mushrooms, and eggs, mixing well.

Warm Blue Cheese Dressing

Yields 1 cup

½ cup Blue Cheese Dressing (see index)
½ cup Pascal's House Dressing (see index)

In a small skillet, combine Blue Cheese Dressing with Vinaigrette, whisking together over low heat until just barely warmed.

To assemble, pour warm dressing over the spinach salad and toss well. Divide onto 4 plates. Sprinkle remaining bacon crumbles over top of tossed salad and top each salad with 3 fried oysters. Serve immediately.

(Photograph by Sam Hanna)

Oysters Francesca

Serves 4

Named for Pascal's mother, Francesca Manale Radosta, the classic Oysters Francesca is a fitting tribute to a grand woman.

Vegetable oil for frying
1 cup corn flour
Salt and pepper to taste
24 raw oysters
4 slices ham, grilled
1 cup Manale Hollandaise Sauce (see index)

Heat 1-1½ inches oil in a deep skillet to 365 degrees. Season corn flour with salt and pepper and lightly dredge oysters in mixture. Fry in hot oil till browned on both sides (about 3 minutes). To assemble, per person, place 6 fried oysters on 1 grilled ham slice, and top with hollandaise sauce.

Oysters Dante

Serves 4

Dante is the name of a street in the Carrollton neighborhood of Uptown New Orleans. It's the first name of Dante Alighieri, Italy's most renowned poet of the Middle Ages, author of the Inferno. *It's also the title of one of Manale's most popular dishes—Oysters Dante. Line cook Carmen Provenzano named the recipe for his son, Dante, and it stuck, long before anyone realized its true provenance!*

2 tbsp. olive oil
8 thin slices prosciutto, julienned
1 leek, thinly sliced on the diagonal
4 tsp. julienned red bell pepper
4 tbsp. julienned red onion
2 tbsp. chopped green onion
1 tbsp. chopped garlic
1 tbsp. chopped parsley
6 tbsp. brandy
¼ cup beef stock
Salt and pepper to taste
½ tsp. crushed red pepper flakes
4 cups penne pasta, cooked
24 large fried oysters

Heat olive oil and sauté prosciutto till browned. Add leeks, bell pepper, red onion, and green onion and sauté together until wilted. Add garlic and parsley and sauté for 1 minute.

Deglaze pan with brandy. Add stock and season with salt, pepper, and red pepper. Bring to a simmer, then add pasta and fried oysters. Adjust seasonings and serve immediately.

(Photograph by Sam Hanna)

(Photograph by Sam Hanna)

Oysters and Spaghetti

Serves 4

This off-menu dish is easy to prepare upon request at Manale's, where the supply of fresh oysters never wanes and the pot of spaghetti is always at a boil.

4 tbsp. butter
6 green onions, finely chopped
4 tbsp. flour
1 cup oyster water
¼ tsp. hot sauce
½ tsp. Lea & Perrins Worcestershire sauce
¼ tsp. white pepper
½ tsp. salt
2 dozen oysters, shucked
1 tbsp. finely chopped parsley
1 1b. spaghetti, cooked

Heat butter in large skillet or saucepan. Add green onions. Cook for 5 minutes.

Slowly whisk in flour. Cook for about 5 minutes. Add oyster water, hot sauce, Worcestershire, white pepper, and salt. Simmer for 5 minutes.

Add oysters and let simmer 5 minutes. Add parsley. Serve over spaghetti.

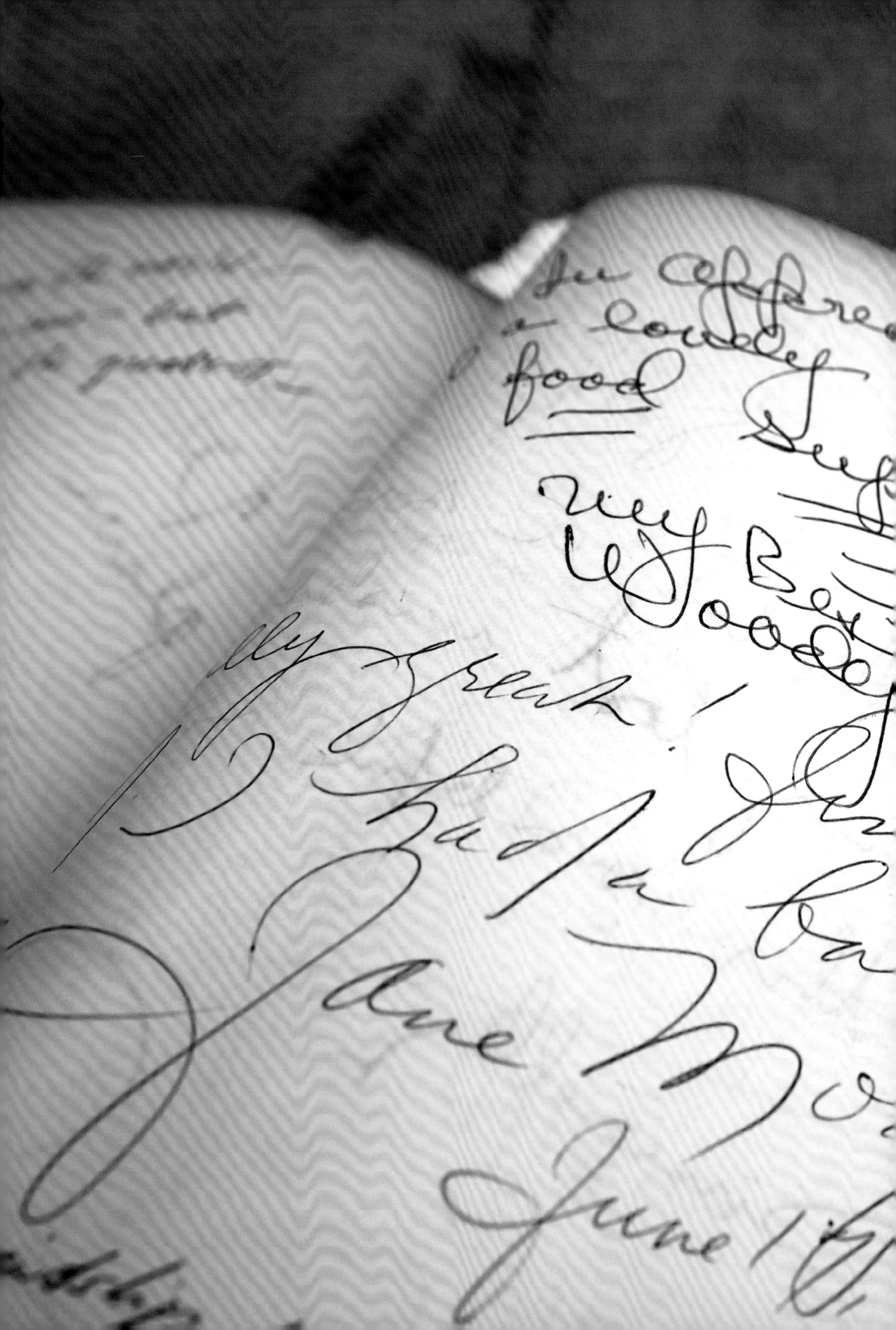
food

Chapter 3
Appetizers

Eggplant Dryades

Serves 4

Although Manale's is located on oak-lined Napoleon Avenue, everyone enters through the side door on Dryades, the Uptown street that follows the curve in the river as it snakes downtown from Jefferson Avenue.

4 tbsp. olive oil
2 lb. raw shrimp, peeled and deveined
6 oz. vodka
1 cup heavy cream
2 garlic cloves, chopped
1 tsp. sugar
½ cup marinara sauce
8-10 basil leaves, chopped
4 tbsp. butter
Salt and pepper to taste
1 egg
1½ cups milk
12 ¼-inch-thick eggplant rounds
2 cups seasoned breadcrumbs
Vegetable oil for frying

(Photograph by Sam Hanna)

Heat olive oil in a skillet. Add shrimp and sauté for 2 minutes until they are pink and firm. Remove from pan and reserve.

Add vodka to skillet and deglaze. Add heavy cream, garlic, and sugar. Bring to a boil and reduce by half.

Add marinara sauce and half of basil. Bring to a simmer and stir in butter. Add remaining basil and return shrimp to skillet. Season with salt and pepper to taste.

Beat egg and milk together to make an egg wash. Dip each eggplant round into the egg wash, then coat well with breadcrumbs. Fry in hot vegetable oil until browned on both sides. To serve, spoon sauce and shrimp over eggplant rounds, 3 rounds per serving.

Stuffed Mushrooms

Serves 4

Jumbo button mushroom caps provide the perfect vessel for claw crabmeat incorporated into a rich dressing. Bright-yellow, fluffy hollandaise sauce delivers the crowning touch.

12 large mushrooms
2 tsp. olive oil
1 stalk celery, chopped
4 tbsp. chopped onion
2 garlic cloves, chopped
¼ tsp. thyme
½ lb. claw crabmeat
½ lb. tiny boiled shrimp
½ cup plain breadcrumbs
Salt and pepper to taste
3 eggs, beaten
1 cup Manale Hollandaise Sauce (see index)

Remove mushroom stems, finely chop, and reserve. In a skillet, bring 1½ inches water to a boil. Add the mushroom caps and poach until tender. Drain and reserve.

Heat olive oil in a skillet. Add chopped mushroom stems, celery, onion, garlic, and thyme. Sauté until mushrooms are browned.

Stir in crabmeat and shrimp. When shrimp are just pink, tighten the mixture with some of the breadcrumbs. Season with salt and pepper.

Stir in eggs, adding more breadcrumbs if needed. Stuff each mushroom cap with about 1 tbsp. filling. Sprinkle lightly with breadcrumbs.

Bake at 350 degrees for 10-15 minutes until heated through and lightly browned. Serve with hollandaise sauce.

(Photograph by Sam Hanna)

Marinated Crab Claws

Serves 4-6

These make a great presentation when prepared and served in clear, glass jars.

½ cup olive oil
¼ cup red wine vinegar
2 tbsp. chopped red onion
1 tbsp. chopped red bell pepper
3 tbsp. white wine
½ tsp. hot sauce
1 tbsp. water
½ tsp. salt
½ tsp. pepper
1 lb. crab claws

Mix marinade well and pour it over crab claws. Marinate in the refrigerator for at least 6 hours. Will remain fresh in the marinade, refrigerated, for up to 48 hours.

Portobello Pizza

Serves 4

This twenty-first-century pizza is fondly remembered by David DeFelice from his days in the kitchen at Manale's.

4 portobello mushrooms, cleaned and
   destemmed
¼ lb. bulk Italian sausage
3 tbsp. chopped onion
1 tbsp. chopped green bell pepper
4 garlic cloves, chopped
¼ cup crawfish tails
¼ cup breadcrumbs, plus 2 tbsp. for topping
¼ cup grated Romano cheese, plus 2 tbsp. for
   topping

Roast or grill mushrooms and reserve. In a skillet, brown the Italian sausage. Add onion, bell pepper, and garlic. Sauté till translucent.

Add the crawfish tails. Stir in breadcrumbs and Romano cheese to tighten. Stuff into mushrooms, sprinkle with additional breadcrumbs and cheese, and bake for 15-20 minutes at 350 degrees till browned.

Crabmeat Ravigote

Serves 4-6

In many New Orleans restaurants, Crabmeat Ravigote is a cold, mayonnaise-based dish,
but the hot, baked Manale version is simply perfection.

1 lb. lump crabmeat
2 tbsp. olive oil
2 garlic cloves, finely chopped
4 tbsp. breadcrumbs
1 tbsp. chopped fresh parsley
¼ tsp. salt

Mix all ingredients together and bake in ramekins or a single baking dish at 325 degrees for 10 minutes until lightly browned.

(Photograph by Sam Hanna)

Crab Cakes

Yields 8 crab cakes

Manale's offers crab cakes as an appetizer, served with remoulade sauce, and as an entrée, topped with additional lump crabmeat and Alfredo sauce.

6 tbsp. butter
1 onion, finely chopped
½ red bell pepper, chopped
½ green bell pepper, chopped
1 stalk celery, chopped
2 garlic cloves, chopped
½ tsp. basil
½ tsp. thyme
¼ tsp. cayenne pepper
2 tsp. salt
1 tsp. hot sauce
1 tsp. Lea & Perrins Worcestershire sauce
8 green onions, chopped
3 tbsp. chopped fresh parsley
1 egg, beaten
¼ lb. claw crabmeat
½ lb. lump crabmeat
1 cup plain breadcrumbs

In a large saucepan, melt butter. Add onion, bell peppers, celery, and garlic. Sauté for 5-7 minutes until soft.

Add basil, thyme, cayenne, and salt. Sauté together for another 3-5 minutes.

Off the heat, add hot sauce, Worcestershire, green onions, and parsley. Stir in egg and crabmeat. Cook over low heat until the egg cooks and tightens the mixture (3-5 minutes). Stir in breadcrumbs to finish.

Form into 3-inch patties about ½ inch thick. The crab cakes may be grilled, deep fried, or lightly sautéed on each side.

(Photograph by Sam Hanna)

Combination Pan Roast

Serves 6-8

Generations of Radosta and DeFelice family members agree that pan roast is their favorite way to begin a meal at Manale's. Although you might expect to see meat in a dish called "pan roast," Manale's version combines nothing but the best seafood from the Gulf of Mexico delivered to the table in a bubbling, hot pan.

8 tbsp. butter
1 green bell pepper, chopped
1 onion, chopped
1 bunch green onions, chopped
1½ tsp. salt
¼ tsp. white pepper
6 tbsp. flour
1 pint raw oysters (oyster water reserved)
1 lb. raw shrimp, peeled and deveined
½ lb. claw crabmeat
½ lb. lump crabmeat
6 tbsp. chopped fresh parsley
1 cup plain breadcrumbs, plus 2 tbsp. for
   topping
¼ cup shrimp stock

Melt butter in a heavy saucepan. Add bell pepper, onion, and green onion. Sauté until translucent. Sprinkle on salt, white pepper, and flour. Cook together for 3-4 minutes.

In a food processor or blender, puree oysters and shrimp. Add to pot and stir together. Remove from heat.

Add crabmeat and parsley. Stir in breadcrumbs. Moisten mixture with oyster water and shrimp stock as needed.

Pour mixture into a baking pan and top with more breadcrumbs. Bake at 350 degrees for 20-25 minutes. Finish under the broiler, for a brown, crispy crust.

(Photograph by Sam Hanna)

Stuffed Artichokes

Serves 4

Pascal's wife, Frances Radosta, often prepared these labor-intensive stuffed artichokes at home for the restaurant. They were always a great favorite with Manale regulars.

4 whole, fresh artichokes
Stuffing (recipe follows)
4 anchovy fillets
4 slices lemon

With a serrated knife, cut off the stem and 1 inch from the top of each artichoke. Stuff each leaf, putting as much stuffing into the top cavity as possible. Arrange 1 anchovy fillet and 1 slice lemon on top of each artichoke.

Place the artichokes in a steamer. Steam the artichokes until tender (about 45 minutes to 1 hour), checking the water level as needed. Serve hot or cold. Store in refrigerator.

Stuffing

8 garlic cloves
1 4-oz. tin anchovies
3 cups seasoned breadcrumbs
¾ cup grated Parmesan cheese
¾ cup grated Romano cheese
¼ cup chopped fresh flat-leaf Italian parsley
1 tbsp. hot sauce
½ cup olive oil

Drop garlic cloves one by one into the food processor with it running. Drain anchovies and put fillets in the food processor. Pulse the garlic and anchovies together to chop.

Add breadcrumbs and cheeses. Pulse to combine well. Pour mixture into a bowl and add parsley. Mix well, then stir in hot sauce and olive oil.

Frances Sansone Radosta (Photograph courtesy of DeFelice Family Collection)

Calamari

Serves 4- 6

The rich, red, Manale Marinara Sauce provides a perfect accent for crispy, fried calamari.

Vegetable oil for deep frying
1 egg
1 cup milk
1 lb. clean squid with tentacles, bodies cut into
    ⅓- to ½-inch-thick rings
2 cups corn flour, seasoned with salt and
    pepper
⅛ tsp. white pepper
⅛ tsp. cayenne pepper
½ tsp. salt
¼ tsp. basil
¼ tsp. oregano
½ tsp. thyme
Lemons, cut into wedges
Salt to taste
1 cup Marinara Sauce (see index)

Pour enough oil into a large, heavy saucepan to reach the depth of 3 inches. Heat over medium heat to 350 degrees.

Make an egg wash by mixing together egg and milk. Add squid to egg wash.

Combine corn flour with seasonings in a bowl. Working in small batches, toss the squid into the corn-flour mixture to coat. Carefully add the squid to the oil and fry until crisp and very pale golden, about 1 minute per batch. Using tongs or a slotted spoon, transfer the fried squid to a paper-towel-lined plate to drain.

Place the fried calamari and lemon wedges on a clean plate. Sprinkle with salt. Serve with Marinara Sauce on side for dipping.

Eggplant Marinara

Serves 4-6

Fried eggplant makes frequent appearances on New Orleans menus, sometimes cut into French-fry-like sticks. At Manale's, rich marinara sauce is often spooned directly on top of thick eggplant disks.

1½ cups milk
1 egg
1 eggplant
2 cups seasoned breadcrumbs
Vegetable oil for frying
1 cup Marinara Sauce (see index)

Make an egg wash by mixing together the milk and egg. Peel eggplant and cut into ¼-inch-thick rounds. Dip each slice in egg wash, then coat with breadcrumbs.

Fry in hot oil till light brown (about 4 minutes). Drain well and serve with marinara sauce.

food

Jelly Break

June 19

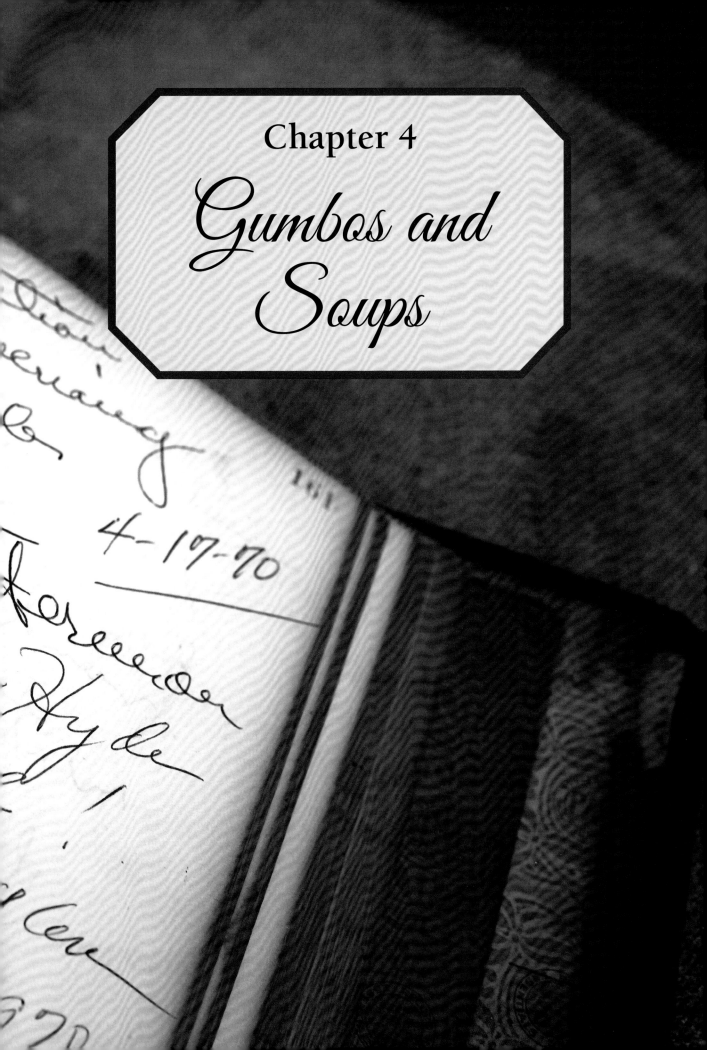

Chapter 4

Gumbos and Soups

Seafood Gumbo

Serves 10-12

Most folks argue that okra and file do not belong together in a gumbo, but at Manale's, they combine for a thick, rich stew.

2 lb. okra, cut in ¼-inch slices
3 tbsp. plus ½ cup vegetable oil
½ cup flour
1 green bell pepper, chopped
4 garlic cloves, chopped
1 onion, chopped
2 stalks celery, chopped
2 qt. seafood stock
2 bay leaves
1 14.5-oz. can crushed tomatoes
1 lb. small raw shrimp, peeled
1 bunch green onions, chopped
3 tbsp. salt
½ tsp. cayenne pepper
½ lb. claw crabmeat
2 tbsp. file powder
½ lb. jumbo lump crabmeat
½ tsp. pepper
Hot sauce to taste
5 cups cooked rice

Preheat oven to 425 degrees. In a large mixing bowl, toss okra with 3 tbsp. oil. Spread in a single layer on a baking sheet and roast for 5 minutes. Stir okra carefully and roast for another 5 minutes. Remove from oven and reserve.

In a 6-qt. stockpot, combine oil and flour, stirring constantly over medium-high heat until roux reaches a chocolate-brown color. Reduce heat to medium and add bell pepper, garlic, onion, and celery. Cook for 10 minutes, stirring occasionally.

Add seafood stock, bay leaves, okra, and tomatoes. Bring to a boil, then reduce to a vigorous simmer. Cook for 1 hour, adding more stock if necessary.

Add shrimp and green onions. Cook for 5 minutes. Add salt, cayenne, and claw crabmeat, and return to a simmer.

Add file powder to a small bowl. Whisk in 1 ladle gumbo liquid to make slurry, then add slurry back to gumbo pot. Fold in jumbo lump crabmeat. Adjust seasonings with pepper and hot sauce. Serve over rice.

(Photograph by Sam Hanna)

Chicken Andouille Gumbo

Serves 10-12

Chicken andouille gumbo is most frequently found in Cajun country but Manale's serves a fine version in the heart of Uptown New Orleans, on Napoleon Avenue.

½ cup oil
½ cup flour
2 stalks celery, chopped
1 onion, chopped
1 green bell pepper, chopped
4 garlic cloves, chopped
2 bay leaves
1 tsp. thyme
3 qt. chicken stock
½ lb. andouille sausage, diced
4 chicken breasts, diced
1 14.5-oz. can whole tomatoes, drained and
  chopped
1 bunch green onions, chopped
4 tbsp. chopped fresh parsley
2 tbsp. file powder
1 tbsp. salt
2 tsp. white pepper
½ tsp. cayenne pepper
1 tsp. hot sauce
5 cups hot rice

In a large, heavy pot, heat oil. Add flour and whisk continually over medium-high heat until roux turns dark brown. Add celery, onion, bell pepper, and garlic. Add bay leaves and thyme.

When vegetables are soft, add stock. Cook for 45 minutes. Skim off excess oil.

Add sausage, chicken, and tomatoes and bring gumbo to a boil. Add green onions, parsley, and file powder. Add salt, white pepper, cayenne pepper, and hot sauce. Serve over rice.

Sweet Potato and Andouille Soup

Serves 10-12

Darrell Keasley is an accomplished cook at Manale's, with New Orleans kitchen traditions running in his veins. His father, Junius Wright, was a celebrated Creole chef in New Orleans restaurants in the 1970s. Darrell is particularly renowned for his soups—always taking the extra step to build complex layers of flavor.

½ lb. andouille sausage
8 medium sweet potatoes, peeled and diced
3 stalks celery, chopped
1 medium onion, chopped
1 medium green bell pepper, chopped
1 tbsp. finely chopped garlic
½ cup white wine
8 cups chicken stock
3 bay leaves
1½ tsp. salt
¼ tsp. ground white pepper
½ tsp. thyme
¼ tsp. oregano
½ tsp. basil
¼ tsp. whole cloves
⅛ tsp. whole allspice
½ tsp. whole black peppercorns

Cut the andouille sausage into rounds, then cut each round into quarters. In a 5-qt. heavy saucepan, brown the andouille in its own renderings. Add half of the diced sweet potatoes. Cook until browned.

Add celery, onion, bell pepper, and garlic. Sauté together until seasoning vegetables begin to brown. Remove mixture from the pan.

Deglaze saucepan with white wine, scraping up all the bits. Return the sautéed sweet-potato mixture to the pan. Add chicken stock, bay leaves, salt, white pepper, thyme, oregano, and basil. Bring to a simmer.

Tie the cloves, allspice, and peppercorns in cheesecloth and add to the pan. Add the remaining raw, diced sweet potatoes to the pan and return to a simmer. Cook until raw potatoes are tender. Remove spice bundle from the pan. Adjust salt and pepper as needed.

Crawfish Bisque

Serves 8-10

Manale's crawfish bisque was so renowned that it even made the Sheboygan Press *news with a report dated September 25, 1963, and headlined: "Crawfish Is King in Old Louisiana." They reported: "Pascal's Manale, one of New Orleans' finest eating places, hedges against natural problems such as drought and cold weather by stocking up when crawfish are plentiful. Jake Radosta opens the doors of two giant freezers. 'We have more than 200 quarts of crawfish bisque in each freezer,' he points out. 'We use them in the off season.'"*

3 lb. whole, boiled crawfish
½ cup butter
¾ cup flour
1 onion, finely chopped
1 green bell pepper, finely chopped
3 stalks celery, finely chopped
2 garlic cloves, finely chopped
½ cup tomato sauce
½ tsp. cayenne pepper
2 tsp. thyme
2 bay leaves
1½ tsp. salt
1 tbsp. Lea & Perrins Worcestershire sauce
1½ qt. crawfish stock (recipe follows)
1 lb. crawfish tails
6 green onions, thinly sliced
2 tbsp. chopped fresh parsley
Stuffed crawfish heads (recipe follows)
¼ cup cooked rice per person

Peel the boiled crawfish. Use the peelings to make crawfish stock.

Melt the butter and whisk in the flour. Stirring constantly over medium-high heat, make a roux by cooking to a deep, golden-brown color. Reduce heat to medium and add onion, bell pepper, celery, and garlic. Continue cooking until seasoning vegetables soften (about 5 minutes). Add tomato sauce and cook for another 5 minutes.

Add cayenne, thyme, bay leaves, salt, and Worcestershire. Whisk in crawfish stock. Simmer together for 20 minutes or more, adding more stock if it becomes too thick.

Add crawfish tails, green onions, and parsley. Simmer for 5 minutes, then add stuffed heads and allow them to heat fully in the bisque. Serve over rice. Include 5-6 heads per bowl and eat by scooping the stuffing out of the heads and eating together with the rice and bisque.

Crawfish Stock

Take all peelings from crawfish, onion, and celery and combine in a stockpot. Cover with 2 qt. water. Bring to a boil and boil vigorously for 10 minutes. Strain.

NOTE: Crawfish stock can be stored in freezer for up to 6 months.

Stuffing

4 tbsp. butter
¼ cup flour
½ onion, finely chopped
1 stalk celery, finely chopped
½ green bell pepper, finely chopped
2 tbsp. tomato paste
¼ tsp. thyme
¼ tsp. pepper
¼ tsp. cayenne pepper
1 tsp. salt
½ lb. crawfish tails, finely chopped
½ cup plain breadcrumbs
1 tbsp. chopped fresh parsley
3 green onions, finely chopped
40-60 cleaned crawfish heads
1 cup seasoned flour for dredging

Melt the butter and whisk in the flour. Stirring constantly over medium-high heat, make a roux by cooking to a deep, golden-brown color.

Reduce heat to medium, add onion, celery, and bell pepper, and continue cooking until seasoning vegetables soften (about 5 minutes).

Whisk in tomato paste, thyme, peppers, and salt. Cook for 3-4 minutes to deepen tomato flavor. Stir in chopped crawfish tails, breadcrumbs, parsley, and green onions. Mix well and remove from heat.

When stuffing is cool enough to handle, stuff cleaned crawfish heads, then roll them in seasoned flour. They may be browned in the oven or pan or deep fried till lightly browned all over.

Friend of Pascal (center, sporting a napkin) spooning stuffing from crawfish head into bisque
(Photograph courtesy of DeFelice Family Collection)

Shrimp Bisque

Serves 10-12

Most bisque soups include cream, but this velvety version is simply redolent with sweet shrimp.

8 tbsp. butter
3 lb. raw shrimp, peeled with shells reserved
2 onions, chopped
1 carrot, chopped
1 stalk celery, chopped
¾ cup brandy
2 gal. water
2 garlic cloves, chopped
½ tsp. thyme
¼ tsp. white pepper
½ cup flour
½ tsp. hot sauce
¼ tsp. salt

Melt 4 tbsp. butter in a stockpot. Sauté the shrimp shells, 1 onion, carrot, and celery for 2 minutes, then flambé with ¼ cup brandy. Cover with 2 gal. water and bring to a boil. Boil vigorously for 45 minutes. Strain and reserve.

In a soup pot, melt 4 tbsp. butter. Add the second onion and chopped garlic. Sauté till translucent.

Sprinkle on thyme and white pepper. Sauté for 1 minute, then flambé with ¼ cup brandy.

Sprinkle flour over sautéed mixture and cook together over medium heat, whisking constantly, until golden brown. Whisk in ½ gal. shrimp stock and bring to a boil. Add peeled shrimp and cook for 2 minutes. Add last ¼ cup brandy. Season with hot sauce and salt and serve.

Crab and Corn Bisque

Serves 10-12

Crab and corn bisque is a perfect summertime soup! Big, fat lumps of blue crab add more sweetness to the fresh corn.

8 tbsp. butter
1 medium onion, chopped
3 stalks celery, chopped
1 medium green bell pepper, chopped
4 tbsp. flour
10 ears fresh corn, shucked and kernels cut
    from ears (reserve cobs for stock)
2 bay leaves
2 tsp. crushed red pepper flakes
½ tsp. salt
½ tsp. thyme
4 qt. crab stock (recipe follows)
1 pint heavy cream
1 tsp. sugar
1 lb. lump crabmeat

In a 5-qt. heavy saucepan, melt butter. Sauté onion, celery, and bell pepper until translucent. Sprinkle flour over sautéed seasoning vegetables. Stir together for 5 minutes until flour is cooked.

Stir in corn, bay leaves, red pepper, salt, and thyme. Add 4 qt. crab stock, whisking constantly. Bring to a boil and redua heavy vigorous simmer. Cook for 25 minutes.

Add heavy cream and sugar. Bring to a simmer and reduce slightly. Stir in crabmeat. Adjust seasonings.

Crab Stock

1 lb. frozen gumbo crabs, coarsely chopped
1 stalk celery, coarsely chopped
Peel of 1 onion
3 garlic cloves
¼ tsp. whole cloves
½ tsp. whole black peppercorns
⅛ tsp. whole allspice
3 bay leaves
10 corn cobs
6 qt. water

In an 8-qt. stockpot, dry sauté the crabs until they change color. Add celery, onion peel, and garlic. Sauté together for 3 minutes.

Tie the cloves, peppercorns, and allspice in cheesecloth and add to the pot with the bay leaves. Add corn cobs. Cover with the water. Bring to a boil and boil vigorously for 20-30 minutes. Strain.

Turtle Soup

Serves 10-12

Alligator meat is sometimes used as a turtle substitute, but at Manale's, there's nothing but freshwater turtles from Louisiana bayous in the soup bowl.

1 lb. turtle meat
1 gal. water
12 tbsp. butter
1 onion, chopped
½ red bell pepper, chopped
3 stalks celery, chopped
2 garlic cloves, chopped
1 6-oz. can tomato puree
½ tsp. thyme
1 tsp. white pepper
1 tbsp. paprika
6 whole cloves
1 tsp. whole allspice
1½ cups dry sherry
2 lemons, zested and juiced
3 hardboiled eggs, finely chopped
¾ cup flour
¼ cup Lea & Perrins Worcestershire sauce
1 tbsp. hot sauce
4 tbsp. finely chopped fresh parsley
Salt to taste

In a stockpot, boil turtle meat in water till tender (about 45 minutes). Drain and reserve stock. Chop the turtle meat to the consistency of shredded chicken and reserve.

In a soup pot, melt 8 tbsp. butter. Add onion, pepper, celery, and garlic. Sauté till translucent.

Whisk in tomato puree. Add thyme, white pepper, and paprika. Stir in stock.

Tie cloves and allspice securely in cheesecloth. Add to the soup pot and bring to a boil, then reduce to a simmer. Add 1 cup sherry and the lemon zest and juice. Cook together for 45 minutes. Remove spice bag. Add the chopped turtle meat and chopped egg.

In a saucepan, melt remaining 4 tbsp. butter, then whisk in flour. Cook over medium-high heat to a blond roux—a light golden brown. Whisk roux into soup, making sure there are no lumps.

Add Worcestershire, hot sauce, and parsley. Add remaining ½ cup sherry. Season with salt to taste.

Savare DeFelice fishing in the bayou.
(Photograph courtesy of DeFelice Family Collection)

Cheese Tortellini Soup

Serves 6-8

This is a favorite from Chef Frank Robinson's time in the kitchen at Manale's.

¾ lb. Italian sausage links, casings removed
1 onion, chopped
6 garlic cloves, chopped
2 qt. chicken stock
2 cups water
1 14.5-oz. can diced tomatoes, undrained
1 tsp. basil
½ tsp. pepper
½ tsp. crushed red pepper flakes
½ tsp. salt
9 oz. fresh tortellini
2 cups shredded, fresh spinach
Grated Romano cheese

In a 5-qt. heavy saucepan, cook and crumble sausage to consistency of ground beef. When sausage begins to brown, add onion and garlic. Cook until onions are golden brown.

Stir in chicken stock, water, and diced tomatoes. Bring to a boil. Add basil, pepper, pepper flakes, and salt.

Add tortellini and return to a boil. Cook for 5 minutes, until almost tender. Stir in spinach and remove from heat. Adjust seasonings and serve with grated Romano cheese.

Chicken and Broccoli Soup
Serves 8-10

The broccoli florets add color, texture, and flavor to this Manale favorite.

4 bone-in chicken breasts
3 broccoli stalks
6 qt. water
3 slices bacon, finely diced
1 onion, peeled and chopped, peels reserved
4 garlic cloves, chopped
½ tsp. thyme
¼ tsp. white pepper
1½ tsp. salt
8 tbsp. butter
½ cup flour
½ tsp. hot sauce
¼ tsp. salt

Debone chicken breasts. Discard the skin and reserve the bones. Cut chicken meat into ¼-inch dice and reserve. Remove the broccoli florets and reserve the florets and stems.

Combine the chicken bones and broccoli stalks in a stockpot and cover with the water. Bring to a boil, then reduce to a simmer and cook, uncovered, for 2 hours, skimming as needed.

In a large soup pot, render the bacon. Add diced chicken and cook briefly. Add onions and garlic and sauté all together until seasoning vegetables are softened. Add thyme, white pepper, and salt.

Strain chicken-broccoli stock and add approximately 3 qt. to the soup pot. Bring all to a boil and simmer vigorously for 25 minutes. Add broccoli florets. Cook until they are just tender (about 8 minutes).

Melt butter in a saucepan. Whisk in flour and cook for 5 minutes over medium heat to a blond roux stage. Gradually whisk roux into simmering soup to thicken. Season with hot sauce and salt.

Split Pea Soup

Serves 10-12

A bit of white wine adds a sophisticated touch to a homegrown favorite, but the last-minute addition of butter takes this split pea soup over the top.

4 tbsp. olive oil
1 lb. ham, diced
3 stalks celery, chopped
1 medium onion, chopped
1 medium green bell pepper, chopped
½ cup white wine
1 lb. dried split peas
1 tsp. crushed red pepper flakes
½ tsp. thyme
8 cups chicken stock
6 tbsp. cold butter
½ tsp. salt
Pepper to taste

In a 5-qt. heavy saucepan, heat olive oil. Brown diced ham. Add celery, onion, and bell pepper. Sauté until they begin to brown.

Add white wine and deglaze the pan, scraping the browned bits from the bottom. Stir in the split peas, red pepper, and thyme. Add chicken stock and bring to a boil. Reduce to a simmer and cook, stirring often to ensure the soup does not stick, for about 45 minutes.

When peas have broken down to a soupy consistency, whip in cold butter by the tablespoon to enrich. Adjust salt and pepper.

Vegetable Beef Soup

Serves 6-8

In most Italian restaurants, a vegetable soup with pasta is often called minestrone. The hearty vegetable beef soup at Manale's includes potatoes with the pasta and is based on the beef brisket that is boiled regularly for Brisket Marinara.

2 cups cooked, shredded beef brisket
10 cups beef stock
1 14.5-oz. can diced tomatoes
1 sweet potato, peeled and cubed
1 Idaho potato, peeled and cubed
1 zucchini squash, cubed
1 yellow squash, cubed
3 carrots, sliced
1 cup cauliflower florets
1 cup broccoli florets
2 tsp. salt
½ tsp. pepper
1 lb. dried spaghetti, broken into 1-2-inch
    pieces
½ lb. fresh spinach, julienned

Bring brisket and beef stock to a boil together in a large soup pot. Add all vegetables except spinach. Boil together for 5 minutes or more until all are just tender. Add salt and pepper.

Add broken spaghetti and boil until al dente. Add spinach leaves and cook until just wilted. Adjust seasonings and serve.

(Photograph by Sam Hanna)

Savare and Virginia DeFelice receive the Louisiana Restaurant Association's "Restaurateur of the Year" award from Miriam Juban, 2004 (Photograph courtesy of DeFelice Family Collection)

Savare's Leek and Potato Soup

Serves 8-10

Despite his full-time work as oyster shucker, Thomas Stewart still prepares the red beans and rice weekly as well as making an occasional soup. Thomas's Potato and Leek Soup was a great favorite of Savare DeFelice, who always called it "Leek and Potato Soup," although usually it's said the other way around.

1 onion, cut in half
8 medium russet potatoes, peeled
½ gal. water
1 tbsp. salt
3 leeks
6 tbsp. butter
6 tbsp. flour
½ cup white wine
1 cup heavy cream
Salt and white pepper to taste

In a large stockpot, combine the onion and 4 potatoes cut in large chunks. Cover with the water and add salt. Bring to a boil and cook vigorously until potatoes break down (about 20 minutes). Remove the onion and discard. Make a potato stock by mashing the potatoes into the cooking liquid.

Cut the remaining 4 potatoes in 1½-inch cubes. Slice the leeks in thin rings, including about 2 inches of the green tops. Rinse thoroughly to remove all dirt.

In a 5-qt. heavy pot, melt butter. Whisk in flour and cook together for 5 minutes until the raw flour taste is gone. Add the stock and white wine. Bring to a boil and add cubed potatoes and sliced leeks. Simmer together briskly until potatoes and leeks become tender (about 8 minutes).

Remove from heat and stir in heavy cream. Season with salt and white pepper and do not allow the soup to boil again.

food

food

June 1

Chapter 5
Sauces, Salads, and Sandwiches

(Photograph by Sam Hanna)

Barbeque Shrimp Sauce

Yields 3 cups

This is my version of barbeque shrimp sauce. Having tasted it side by side with Manale's, I have to say that, to my taste, they are very, very similar. It's no secret that originally, Manale's was made with margarine. America developed a serious taste for margarine during World War II rationing, eventually preferring it to butter. That undoubtedly is why Pascal Radosta used it in his original recipe, but now, Manale's uses a butter/margarine blend. Margarine also holds up to the high heat needed to cook barbeque shrimp better than real butter, which can easily burn. The original Manale barbeque shrimp are baked in a 500-degree convection oven for five to seven minutes. I cook mine under a broiler for about ten minutes, stirring the pan thoroughly at the five-minute mark.

1½ lb. butter
3 lemons
12 whole garlic cloves, peeled
1 tbsp. pepper
1 tbsp. white pepper
1 tbsp. cayenne pepper
1 tbsp. sweet Hungarian paprika
1½ tbsp. salt
½ tsp. celery seed
1 tsp. dry mustard
¼ tsp. ground ginger
6 whole pods coriander, crushed
4 bay leaves
3 tbsp. Lea & Perrins Worcestershire sauce

Melt butter in a saucepan. Peel wide strips of skin from lemons. Juice the lemons and discard the remaining fruit. Add peel strips and juice to melted butter.

Add all remaining ingredients and bring to a boil. Remove from heat immediately. Cool at room temperature. Store in refrigerator. Strain sauce before using.

NOTE: This is enough barbeque sauce for 3 lb. large, head-on shrimp. Combine shrimp and sauce, and broil as described above.

(Photograph by Sam Hanna)

Marinara Sauce

Yields 6 cups

Anchovies and red wine are the two ingredients that make Manale's Marinara Sauce a real standout.

¼ cup olive oil
1 4-oz. tin anchovies
8 garlic cloves, chopped
1 onion, chopped
3 stalks celery, chopped
1 tsp. thyme
½ tsp. white pepper
1 tsp. salt
1 lb. 12 oz. can whole roma tomatoes and juice
1 cup water
1 cup red wine
2 cups chicken stock

In a 5-qt. saucepan, heat olive oil. Add anchovies and sauté, stirring constantly until they begin to brown and break up. Add garlic, onion, and celery. Sauté until translucent. Add thyme, white pepper, and salt.

Add roma tomatoes, crushing each by hand as it goes into the pan. Add tomato juice. Rinse tomato can with 1 cup water and add to the pan.

Add red wine and chicken stock. Bring to a boil, then reduce to a simmer. Cook together for 45 minutes to 1 hour, stirring periodically. Can be frozen for 6-8 months.

Red Gravy

Yields 6 cups

All across America, Italians carry on the debate—"Is it sauce or gravy?" Sicilian New Orleanians usually call their spaghetti sauce "red gravy." Since it uses the traditional celery, bell pepper, and onion of the Creole mirepoix, many even start their red gravy by making a dark, New Orleans roux! Here is the Manale version as passed down through the generations. Take note of their secret ingredient, four links of Italian sausage! The sausage stews in the red gravy as it simmers but never sees the dining room. Before the red gravy hits the line, the sausage is removed from the pot and eaten separately as a secret treat for the Manale kitchen's cooks.

¼ cup olive oil
4 links Italian sausage
2 stalks celery, chopped
1 green bell pepper, chopped
1 onion, chopped
2 garlic cloves, chopped
½ tsp. thyme
1 tbsp. basil
1 tsp. oregano
2 tbsp. salt
1 tbsp. white pepper
1 lb. 12 oz. can tomato puree
1 lb. 12 oz. can crushed tomatoes
1 6-oz. can tomato paste
4 cups beef stock
4 cups water
¾ cups grated Romano cheese
¼ cup sugar
4 tbsp. Lea & Perrins Worcestershire sauce

Heat olive oil in stockpot. Brown sausage. Remove from pot.

Add celery, pepper, onion and garlic and cook slowly until caramelized. Add thyme, basil, oregano, salt, and pepper, stirring well. Add tomato puree, crushed tomatoes, tomato paste, beef stock, and water.

Return the sausages to the pot. Bring to a boil, then lower the heat. Simmer for 1½ hours, stirring frequently to make sure the sauce doesn't stick.

Add the grated Romano cheese and simmer for another ½ hour. Add sugar and simmer for another ½ hour. Add Worcestershire and simmer for another ½ hour.

Remove sausage and serve separately. Sauce may be stored in refrigerator for up to 3 days. It may be frozen for up to 1 year.

(Photograph by Sam Hanna)

Creole Sauce

Yields 10 cups

Creole sauce is the base of shrimp creole, but at Manale's, chicken cacciatore is stewed in creole sauce instead of the more predictable marinara or red gravy. The julienned vegetables, instead of the usual chopped seasonings, give a special texture and appearance to the sauce.

4 tbsp. olive oil
1 large onion, julienned
3 stalks celery, julienned
6 green onions, julienned
8 garlic cloves, julienned
2 bay leaves
1 tsp. thyme
2 tsp. oregano
½ tsp. paprika
½ tsp. cayenne pepper
1 lb. 12 oz. can whole tomatoes
1 14.5-oz. can tomato puree
4 cups shrimp stock
2 tbsp. cornstarch
4 tbsp. cold water

In a 5-qt. heavy saucepan, heat olive oil. Add onions, celery, green onions, and garlic. Sauté for 3-5 minutes till just tender.

Add bay leaves, thyme, oregano, paprika, cayenne pepper, tomato products, and shrimp stock. Bring to a boil, then reduce heat and simmer vigorously for 15 minutes.

In separate container, mix cornstarch and water. Whisk into sauce. Bring to a boil and simmer for 5 minutes until thickened. Store in refrigerator for up to 3 days. It may be frozen for up to 1 year.

Manale Béarnaise Sauce

Yields 1¼ cups

Piquant capers join green onions and anise-flavored tarragon in a rich butter sauce that's a favorite accompaniment to steaks and chops.

2 tsp. dried tarragon leaves
1 tbsp. capers, drained and chopped
6 green onions, thinly sliced
¼ cup red wine vinegar
2 egg yolks
1 lemon, juiced
8 oz. clarified butter
¼ tsp. salt
⅛ tsp. white pepper
Hot sauce to taste

Combine tarragon leaves, capers, green onions, and red wine vinegar in a saucepan. Bring to a boil and reduce by half. Cool thoroughly.

In the top of a double boiler, combine vinegar mixture with eggs and lemon juice. Whisk vigorously over lightly boiling water until thickened and pale yellow. Slowly whisk in butter. Season with salt, pepper, and hot sauce and keep warm in top of double boiler until ready to serve.

(Photograph by Sam Hanna)

Manale Hollandaise Sauce

Yields 1 cup

A little red wine vinegar and Louisiana-style hot sauce adds zing to the sunny-yellow Manale Hollandaise Sauce.

2 egg yolks
1 lemon, juiced
2 tbsp. red wine vinegar
8 oz. clarified butter
¼ tsp. salt
⅛ tsp. white pepper
Hot sauce to taste

In the top of a double boiler, combine egg yolks, lemon juice, and vinegar. Whisk constantly over lightly boiling water until mixture thickens and is a light lemon color. Slowly drizzle in melted butter, continuously whisking. Add salt and pepper, and whisk in 2-3 shots of hot sauce. Keep warm over the double boiler until ready to serve.

Alfredo Sauce

Yields 1½ cups

This thick, rich, creamy sauce is used both as a pasta sauce and to sauce succulent crab cakes. At Manale's, Alfredo sauce is always made to order.

8 tbsp. butter
1 cup heavy cream
1½ cups grated Romano cheese
¼ cup fresh parsley

Melt butter in a medium saucepan over medium-low heat. Add cream and simmer for 5 minutes. Add cheese and whisk quickly, heating through. Stir in parsley and serve.

Demi-Glace

Yields 1 cup

This is a sauce usually reserved for professional kitchens but can be accomplished successfully in any home kitchen.

3 tbsp. plus 1 tbsp. butter
4 tbsp. flour
3 cups veal or beef stock
1 tbsp. Lea & Perrins Worcestershire sauce
Salt and pepper to taste

In a saucepan over medium-high heat, whisk together 3 tbsp. butter and the flour until flour is just cooked, 3-4 minutes. Whisk in 1 cup stock and bring to a boil, whisking occasionally. Reduce by half.

In a separate saucepan, boil remaining 2 cups stock with Worcestershire sauce until reduced by half. Whisk together the sauce and reduced stock, allowing to reduce again by half. Season with salt and pepper to taste. Whisk the remaining 1 tbsp. butter into the sauce to enrich it. Hold in a water bath till ready to serve.

Cocktail Sauce

Yields 1½ cups

Everyone at Manale's oyster bar mixes their own version of cocktail sauce to enjoy with freshly shucked oysters. When Manale's Combination Remoulade appetizer arrives in the dining room, this is the special recipe used to contrast Manale's spicy, white remoulade sauce.

1 cup ketchup
4 tbsp. Lea & Perrins Worcestershire sauce
1 tbsp. hot sauce
1 stalk celery, finely ground
2 tbsp. prepared horseradish
1 tbsp. sugar

Mix all ingredients together and store in refrigerator for up to 2 weeks.

Pascal's Spicy Mayonnaise

Yields 1 cup

Another legacy of Pascal, this spicy mayonnaise provides the base for many delicious dressings and sauces, most significantly the distinctive Manale remoulade. Chef Mark DeFelice remembers learning this family secret from his uncle Jake Radosta.

1 egg
1½ tbsp. Colman's dry mustard
1 lemon, juiced
1 cup vegetable oil
¼ tsp. salt

Combine egg, dry mustard, and lemon juice in a food processor. Process for about 30 seconds until light yellow. With processor running, slowly dribble in the vegetable oil until the mayonnaise becomes white and thickened. Sprinkle in the salt and pulse again a couple of times to thoroughly combine. Store in refrigerator for up to 1 week.

(Photograph by Sam Hanna)

Remoulade Sauce

Yields 1¼ cups

Chopped green olives add a distinctive Sicilian note to Manale's remoulade sauce. The cold, mayonnaise-based sauce is a New Orleans classic used to dress luscious lumps of crabmeat or spicy boiled shrimp.

1 cup Pascal's Spicy Mayonnaise (see index)
1 tbsp. chopped green olives
2 tbsp. finely chopped green onions
1 tsp. chopped celery
1 hardboiled egg, chopped
1 tbsp. chopped dill pickle
1 tbsp. Creole mustard
1 tsp. A1 steak sauce
2 tsp. Lea & Perrins Worcestershire sauce

Mix all ingredients together and use to sauce boiled shrimp or crabmeat. Store in refrigerator for up to 1 week.

(Photograph by Sam Hanna)

Tartar Sauce

Yields 1 cup

Pascal's special spicy mayonnaise is the base for Manale's unparalleled tartar sauce, made there fresh daily.

1 cup Pascal's Spicy Mayonnaise (see index)
3 tbsp. finely chopped dill pickle relish
1 tsp. finely chopped red bell pepper
1 tsp. finely chopped green bell pepper

Mix all together and store in refrigerator for up to 1 week.

Mignonette Sauce

Yields ½ cup

As its name suggests, mignonette sauce hails from France, where it provides a subtle piquancy to their famous Belon oysters. It's a relative newcomer to the Crescent City, but if asked, "Uptown T," the oyster shucker, can whip one up for you!

1 tbsp. coarsely ground fresh white or black
    peppercorns (or to taste)
½ cup white or red wine vinegar
2 tbsp. finely chopped shallots or sweet onions
Salt to taste

Mix together and chill.

Balsamic Vinaigrette

Yields 1½ cups

Balsamic vinegar did not become popular among Sicilian New Orleanians until the latter part of the twentieth century, when it became readily available. This traditional, aged ingredient from Modena, Italy is carefully crafted from grape must. When it comes to balsamic, the older the better, as aging distills the liquid into a thick, semisweet nectar used in both sweet and savory ways in its Italian homeland.

4 tbsp. balsamic vinegar
2 tbsp. red wine vinegar
¼ tsp. dried oregano
2 garlic cloves, chopped
2 tsp. chopped fresh basil
¼ tsp. sugar
¼ tsp. salt
⅛ tsp. white pepper
1 cup olive oil

Combine the vinegars in a 1-qt. bowl. Whisk in the oregano, garlic, basil, sugar, salt, and pepper. Whisking continuously, add the olive oil in a slow stream until dressing is thickened. Store in refrigerator for up to 3 days.

Creamy Italian House Dressing

Yields 1½ cups

With the slight sweetness that Sicilian Americans love, Manale's house dressing has been a favorite for decades.

2 tbsp. chopped onion
1 garlic clove
1 tsp. sugar
2 tbsp. red wine vinegar
1 tbsp. water
¼ cup olive oil
1 cup Pascal's Spicy Mayonnaise (see index)
1 tsp. sweet basil
2 tsp. finely chopped red bell pepper

In a blender or food processor, combine onion, garlic, sugar, vinegar, and water. Mix till smooth. With processor running, slowly pour in olive oil.

Put mayonnaise in a mixing bowl and slowly whisk in vinaigrette mixture. Whisk in basil and red bell pepper. Refrigerate overnight to allow flavors to marry. Store in refrigerator for up to 1 week.

"Miss Bev" Simon (Photograph by Sam Hanna)

Pascal's Salad

Serves 4

Virginia DeFelice, Pascal's daughter, had her own special salad that she enjoyed for lunch everyday at Manale's, accompanied by crisp Saltine crackers generously spread with margarine—not butter! Virginia's salad was composed simply of chopped, blanched vegetables, which she dressed at the table with oil and vinegar. The salad named for her dad has more of a traditional Italian bent.

4 cups lettuce greens
4 green bell pepper rings
12 marinated artichoke hearts
4 tomato wedges
12 black olives
12 anchovies
Pascal's House Dressing (recipe follows)

Place greens either in a communal bowl or individual bowls. Decorate the top with pepper rings, artichoke hearts, tomatoes, olives, and anchovies, then dress with Pascal's House Dressing.

Pascal's House Dressing

Yields 3½ cups

1 cup olive oil
2 cups red wine vinegar
1½ tbsp. Creole mustard
2 tbsp. finely chopped green onions
1 garlic clove, finely chopped
1 tbsp. oregano
2 tbsp. salt
2 tbsp. pepper

Use blender to mix together all ingredients. Chill before using. Will keep refrigerated for up to 1 week.

Pascal Radosta (Photograph by Sam Hanna)

Blue Cheese Dressing

Yields 2 cups

Use creamy, piquant Italian gorgonzola to make this blue cheese dressing zing.

¼ cup Pascal's Spicy Mayonnaise (see index)
¼ cup sour cream
6 tbsp. light cream
2 tsp. Lea & Perrins Worcestershire sauce
½ tbsp. hot sauce
1 cup crumbled blue cheese

Whisk together mayonnaise, sour cream, light cream, Worcestershire, and hot sauce until smooth. Fold in blue cheese. Store in refrigerator for up to 1 week.

(Photograph by Sam Hanna)

Insalata Manale

Serves 1

This is Manale's version of what was once popularly called a "wop salad" in New Orleans. "Wop" stood for "With Out Papers," an ugly term sometimes used to refer to Italian immigrants. You can be sure that name was never applied to a Manale Italian salad!

1½ cups coarsely chopped iceberg lettuce
½ cup olive salad
4-5 tomato wedges
¼ cup diced mozzarella cheese
3 giardiniera peppers
6-8 kalamata olives
3-4 artichoke hearts
4 tbsp. grated Romano cheese

Toss lettuce together with olive salad and spoon onto plate. Garnish greens with tomatoes, mozzarella cheese, giardiniera peppers, kalamata olives, and artichoke hearts. Sprinkle Romano cheese on top and serve.

(Photograph by Sam Hanna)

Italian Olive Salad

Yields approximately 3½ cups

Rich, oily olive salad is an essential ingredient on a muffaletta sandwich. At Manale's, it dresses the lettuce base of their classic Insalata Manale.

2 tbsp. red wine vinegar
¼ cup extra virgin olive oil
1 tsp. dried oregano
½ tsp. cracked black pepper
1 cup pimento-stuffed green olives, drained
    and coarsely chopped
⅓ cup marinated artichoke hearts, coarsely
    chopped with marinade
½ cup canned chickpeas, drained and coarsely
    chopped
1 cup cocktail onions, drained and coarsely
    chopped
½ cup giardiniera vegetables, drained and
    coarsely chopped
1 tbsp. capers, drained and coarsely chopped
2 garlic cloves, chopped

Make vinaigrette by whisking together red wine vinegar and olive oil. Add oregano and black pepper and reserve. In a large bowl, mix together the remaining ingredients.

Pour vinaigrette over vegetables and mix well. Cover tightly and marinate for at least 8 hours, preferably overnight, stirring occasionally. Store in refrigerator for up to 1 week.

Honey Mustard Dressing

Yields 2 cups

The Manale's version of honey mustard salad dressing originated at Visko's restaurant on the west bank of New Orleans, where Chef Mark DeFelice worked with "Miss Bev" Simon back in the 1980s.

1 cup Pascal's Spicy Mayonnaise (see index)
4 tbsp. yellow mustard
½ cup Creole mustard
¼ cup honey
4 tbsp. white vinegar
2 lemons, juiced
1½ tbsp. Colman's dry mustard
⅛ tsp. cayenne pepper
½ tsp. white pepper

Combine mayonnaise, yellow mustard, Creole mustard, and honey. Mix well. In a separate bowl mix white vinegar, lemon juice, dry mustard, cayenne, and white peppers until smooth. Whisk the vinegar mixture into the mayonnaise mixture. Store in refrigerator for up to 1 week.

Manale's Seasoned Breadcrumbs

Yields 2½ cups

This special mix of seasoned breadcrumbs provides an Italian touch for breading fried food or tightening up stuffings and dressings. Progresso seasoned Italian breadcrumbs are an authentic substitution. After all, that famous Italian food maker is a New Orleans original.

2 cups dried breadcrumbs
2 tsp. thyme
1 tsp. oregano
1 tsp. basil
½ tsp. garlic powder
½ tsp. onion powder
½ cup grated Romano cheese

Mix together. Store tightly sealed in refrigerator.

(Photograph by Sam Hanna)

Barbeque Shrimp Poorboy

Serves 4

The poorboy sandwich is a New Orleans invention. Born of necessity during the 1929 streetcar strike, the sandwich was designed as a loaf, large enough to feed a family. Benny and Clovis Martin of Martin Brothers Grocery had great sympathy for the striking streetcar drivers, who were unable to feed themselves and their families as the long, violent strike dragged on. They posted signs all over town stating that, as long as the strike lasted, "those poor boys would find a free meal at Martin's." Most frequently, the free three-foot-long sandwiches consisted of fried potatoes and roast-beef gravy. Manale's opulent barbeque shrimp poorboy is a relative newcomer, having arrived in the 1980s.

2 36-inch loaves French bread
1 cup Barbeque Shrimp Sauce (see index)
1½ lb. small, peeled raw shrimp

Cut each French bread loaf in half crosswise, resulting in 4 18-inch lengths of bread. Keep the round ends intact. Warm the 4 half-loaves until just crusty.

While the bread is warming, heat barbeque sauce and add shrimp, cooking gently until shrimp are firm and just cooked (5 minutes or less). Using the handle of a wooden spoon, and working from the open, cut end of the bread, make a cavity down the center of each bread half, still keeping the round end intact. Ladle in barbeque shrimp and sauce. Serve with extra sauce for dipping.

(Photograph by Sam Hanna)

(Photograph by Sam Hanna)

D'Antoni Sandwich

Serves 1

Dr. Joseph D'Antoni was a lifelong friend of Pascal's who regularly enjoyed a good high-stakes card game in Pascal's office at Manale's, fueled by his favorite, hot ham poorboy sandwich.

½ loaf poorboy bread
8 oz. sliced ham
4 oz. sliced cheddar
Lettuce and tomato for dressing

Assemble sandwich. Place on grill and press down with a weight. Cook for 2-3 minutes, turn over, and cook on other side.

Seated at the far right is Dr. Joseph D'Antoni, Pascal's gambling buddy, for whom this sandwich was named. (Photograph by DeFelice Family Collection)

Peteburger

Serves 4

Pete Radosta began working at his uncle Frank Manale's restaurant at a very early age, and except for his time in the service, Pete was always there. Karry Byrd, a forty-plus-year Manale veteran, remembers personally making Pete's special burger for him.

1 lb. ground beef
2 tbsp. Lea & Perrins Worcestershire sauce
4 tbsp. tomato juice
2 eggs, beaten
¼ cup breadcrumbs
½ tsp. salt
¼ tsp. pepper

Mix together. Divide mixture into fourths. Form into patties and cook to desired doneness. Serve with lettuce, tomato, onion, and Pascal's Spicy Mayonnaise (see index).

food

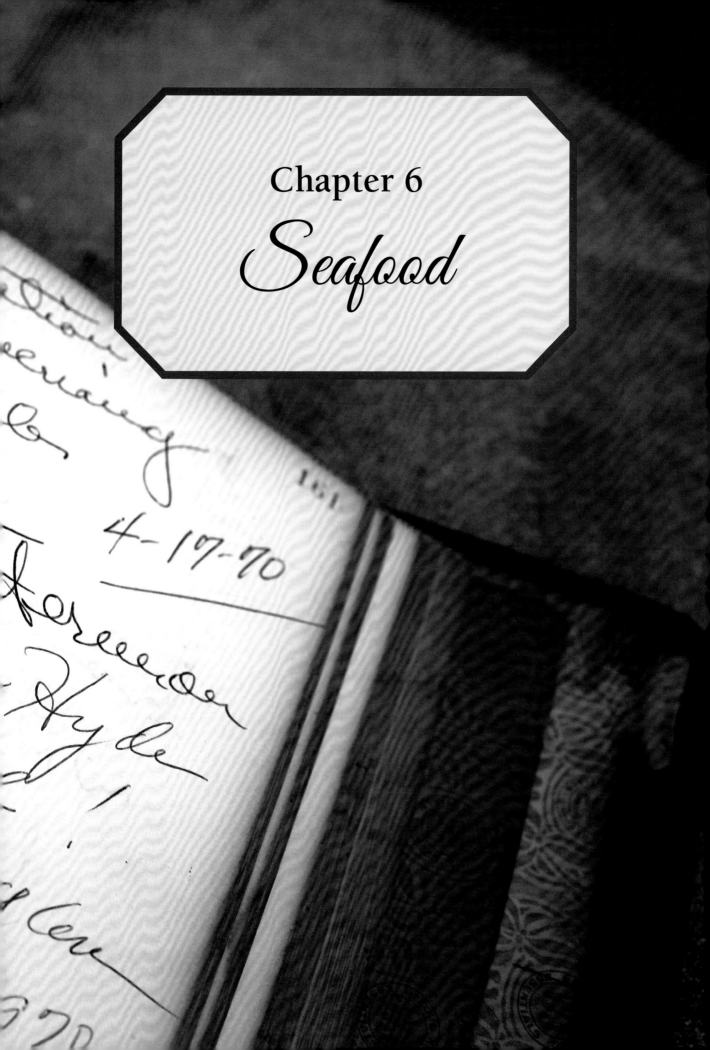

Chapter 6
Seafood

(Photograph by Sam Hanna)

Mark's Barbeque Shrimp

Serves 4

The original barbeque shrimp recipe as created by Pascal Radosta in 1954 is a tightly guarded family secret, but Mark DeFelice likes to make this version at home. The head-on shrimp always used in the restaurant version (and in most other recipes) are often hard to find fresh in landlocked areas. Mark uses headless shrimp, making this easy to reproduce anywhere. Heat up some French bread and get ready for sopping up the rich sauce. You won't want to miss a drop!

1 lb. or 21-25 headless raw shrimp
Manale Spice Mix (recipe follows)
½ tsp. chopped garlic
½ cup Lea & Perrins Worcestershire sauce
¼ tsp. hot sauce
¾ cup olive oil
½ cup white wine

Wash and pat dry shrimp. Add Manale Spice Mix, garlic, Worcestershire, and hot sauce. Pour olive oil over shrimp, and add white wine. Stir together.

Cook over high heat until shrimp are done, approximately 10 minutes. Do not overcook shrimp. Serve shrimp in a wide soup bowl with hard-crust French bread for dipping in the peppery sauce.

Manale Spice Mix

4 tsp. pepper
½ tsp. cayenne pepper
1 tsp. paprika
1 tsp. salt
1 tsp. thyme
1 tsp. oregano
1 tsp. dried basil

Combine all ingredients.

Shrimp a la Scarpia

Serves 4

Baron Scarpia is a major character in Puccini's opera Tosca. *This Manale creation was undoubtedly named by opera lover Frances Radosta DeFelice.*

5 tbsp. butter
¼ cup flour
1½ cups milk
1 cup chicken stock
6 garlic cloves, chopped
4 tbsp. chopped fresh parsley
Salt and white pepper to taste
24 large raw shrimp, peeled and deveined
1 lb. spaghetti, cooked

In a 3-qt. saucepan over medium heat, melt 4 tbsp. butter. Whisk in flour, stirring constantly until flour is cooked, 3-4 minutes. Whisk in milk and chicken stock. Add garlic, parsley, salt, and white pepper. Simmer together until sauce thickens.

In a skillet, melt the remaining 1 tbsp. butter. Sauté shrimp for 3-4 minutes until they are cooked. Pour sauce over shrimp, and turn spaghetti in sauce. Serve with more sauce on top.

Shrimp and Grits

Serves 4

Shrimp and grits is not a New Orleans original. It arrived from Charleston, South Carolina in the 1980s and has become a staple here. Manale's Barbeque Shrimp Sauce makes their version completely unique.

1 cup Barbeque Shrimp Sauce (see index)
2 lb. medium raw peeled shrimp
4 green onions, thinly sliced
Salt, pepper, and hot sauce to taste
Hot grits

Heat barbeque sauce in a sauteuse pan over medium heat. Stir in shrimp and gently poach in the sauce until shrimp are firm and pink. Add the green onions and cook for 3 minutes. Adjust seasonings with salt, pepper, and hot sauce. Serve over hot grits.

Shrimp Tre Formaggi

Serves 4-6

The traditional Italian cheeses—Parmesan, Romano, and mozzarella—have been staples of the Manale kitchen since 1913. During his tenure there, Chef Mark DeFelice added the sharp accent of feta to some dishes, an unusual touch in Sicilian-New Orleans food.

¼ cup olive oil
2 lb. peeled and deveined raw shrimp
3 garlic cloves, chopped
6 green onions, chopped
¼ cup brandy
Salt, pepper, and crushed red pepper flakes to taste
½ cup shrimp stock
4 tbsp. butter
½ cup heavy cream
¼ cup crumbled feta cheese
¼ cup grated mozzarella cheese
¼ cup grated Romano cheese
1 lb. linguine, cooked
3 tbsp. chopped fresh parsley
¼ tsp. paprika

In medium sauté pan, heat olive oil. Add shrimp and sauté over high heat, for 2-3 minutes. Stir in garlic and green onions, then deglaze pan with brandy. Season with salt and peppers and add stock.

Bring to a boil, then whisk in butter. Add cream and reduce heat to a simmer. Add all 3 cheeses.

When cheeses melt, add cooked pasta. Re-season to taste. Serve garnished with parsley and paprika.

Shrimp Savare

Serves 4

Savare DeFelice—or "Paw Paw," as Manale's fifth generation affectionately called him—preferred his shrimp served in a simple sauté with crispy Brabant potatoes.

4 tbsp. butter
¼ cup chopped onion
3 tbsp. chopped celery
2 tbsp. chopped red bell pepper
1 lb. medium raw shrimp, peeled and deveined
¼ cup white wine
4 tbsp. shrimp stock
1 cup Brabant Potatoes (see index)
Salt and pepper to taste

Melt butter in a 10-inch sauté pan. Add onion, celery, and red pepper. Sauté together for about 3 minutes, until the seasoning vegetables are tender but still have texture.

Add shrimp and sauté for 1 minute. Add white wine and stock and stir together well. Bring to a boil, and then add Brabant potatoes. Season with salt and pepper, and serve.

(Photograph by Sam Hanna)

Shrimp Creole

Serves 4

From fine, white-tablecloth establishments to humble lunch counters, shrimp creole is a standard on New Orleans menus. Manale's version stands out with julienned slices of seasoning vegetables providing a texture very different from the usual smooth red-gravy versions.

4 tbsp. olive oil
1 medium onion, julienned
2 stalks celery, julienned
½ green bell pepper, julienned
6 garlic cloves, thinly sliced
½ tsp. thyme
¼ tsp. paprika
2 bay leaves
1 cup shrimp stock
1 14.5-oz. can diced tomatoes and juice
2 lb. medium raw shrimp, peeled and deveined
3 tbsp. butter
3 tbsp. flour
Salt and white pepper to taste
Cooked rice

Heat olive oil in a skillet. Add onion, celery, bell pepper, and garlic. Sauté until just soft.

Add thyme, paprika, and bay leaves. Sauté for 1 minute and add shrimp stock. Bring to a boil.

Add tomatoes and juice. Reduce to a vigorous simmer. Cook together for 20 minutes.

Add shrimp and cook for 3 minutes. In a skillet, melt butter and whisk in flour. Cook for 2-3 minutes to blond roux stage.

Whisk in blond roux to thicken. Season sauce with salt and white pepper. Serve over cooked rice.

Shrimp Diavolo

Serves 4   ·

Diavolo sauces often include chili peppers. At Manale's, only crushed red pepper flakes add a devilish touch to this traditional Italian dish, which translates as "shrimp of the devil."

3 tbsp. olive oil
3 lb. raw shrimp, peeled and deveined
1 lb. mushrooms, sliced
8 green onions, sliced
2 garlic cloves, chopped
1 tbsp. crushed red pepper flakes
4 oz. brandy
1 cup Marinara Sauce (see index)
½ cup shrimp stock
4 tbsp. cold butter, lightly tossed in flour
Salt and pepper to taste
1 lb. fettuccine noodles, cooked

Heat olive oil in a sauteuse pan. Sauté shrimp for 1 minute, then add mushrooms, green onions, garlic, and crushed red pepper. Deglaze with brandy and flambé.

Add marinara sauce and shrimp stock. Bring to a boil. Whisk in butter by the tablespoon to thicken. Season sauce with salt and pepper. Serve with fettuccine.

(Photograph by Sam Hanna)

(Photograph by Sam Hanna)

Shrimp Mediterranean

Serves 4

Chef Mark DeFelice's favorite, feta cheese, accompanies the Mediterranean touch of kalamata olives in this brilliantly colored pasta dish.

2 tbsp. olive oil
8 thin slices prosciutto
18 raw jumbo shrimp, peeled and deveined
¼ cup dry white wine
¼ tsp. salt
⅛ tsp. pepper
¼ tsp. crushed red pepper flakes
6 basil leaves, sliced into a thin chiffonade
6 garlic cloves, chopped
18 roasted garlic cloves
3 green onions, sliced
8-10 pitted kalamata black olives
2 tbsp. diced roasted red pepper
½ lb. fresh spinach
¼ cup shrimp stock
1½ tbsp. lemon juice
4 tbsp. cold butter, lightly tossed in flour
¼ cup small-diced feta cheese, plus 2 tbsp. for
    topping
¼ cup grated Romano cheese
1 tbsp. chopped fresh parsley
1 lb. penne pasta, cooked

Heat oil in sauté pan. Add prosciutto and render it, allowing it to begin to brown. Add shrimp. Cook for 1-2 minutes.

Deglaze pan with white wine. Add salt, pepper, crushed red pepper, basil, garlic, green onions, black olives, roasted pepper, spinach, and shrimp stock. Simmer for 2-3 minutes.

Add lemon juice. Remove from heat and whisk in butter. Toss in feta, Romano, parsley, and pasta. Sprinkle with feta before serving.

Frutti di Mare

Serves 4-6

Frutti di mare *literally means "fruit of the sea." Succulent lobster tails and giant, tender scallops, jewels of the Atlantic Ocean, are combined with shrimp, crab, and oysters from the Gulf of Mexico to make the Manale version of this seafood-pasta classic uniquely theirs.*

6 tbsp. olive oil
1 lobster tail meat, cubed
3 large scallops
12 jumbo raw shrimp, peeled
½ cup dry white wine
¼ tsp. pepper
½ tsp. white pepper
½ tsp. salt
1 tbsp. crushed red pepper flakes
2 garlic cloves, chopped
6 green onions, chopped
½ cup shrimp stock
2 cups Marinara Sauce (see index)
12 shucked oysters with oyster water
1 lb. jumbo lump crabmeat
2 tbsp. chopped fresh parsley
1 lb. spaghetti, cooked

Heat oil in skillet. Sear lobster, scallops, and shrimp until lightly browned, then reserve them while you deglaze the pan with white wine. Add pepper, white pepper, salt, crushed red pepper, garlic, green onions, and shrimp stock. Bring to a boil, then simmer for 3-4 minutes.

Add marinara sauce and return to a simmer. Add oysters and oyster water, then return seafood to pan. Add crabmeat and parsley. Heat spaghetti in sauce. To serve, roll spaghetti onto a plate. Arrange the individual pieces of seafood on top, and finish with the sauce.

(Photographs by Sam Hanna)

(Photograph by Sam Hanna)

Stuffed Eggplant

Serves 6-8

An old Manale menu described their version of stuffed eggplant as "an ancient family recipe." The Sicilian love of eggplant dates back to the 1300s, when the dark purple, oval vegetable first arrived there with the Arabs. In New Orleans, the love affair continues as Gulf shrimp and crabmeat dress up the eggplant, with a bit of ham as contrast. A meal in itself, it's also a great side dish for any roasted meat.

2 medium eggplant, peeled and cubed
4 tbsp. olive oil
1 cup cubed ham
2 onions, chopped
3 stalks celery, chopped
6 garlic cloves, chopped
1 tsp. thyme
½ tsp. oregano
1 lb. small raw shrimp, peeled
¼ cup grated Romano cheese
½ lb. claw crabmeat
4 eggs, beaten
¼ tsp. cayenne pepper
½ tsp. white pepper
1½ tsp. salt
8 green onions, chopped
¾ cup plain breadcrumbs
½ lb. jumbo lump crabmeat
¼ cup plain breadcrumbs
2 tbsp. butter

Boil and drain eggplant. Reserve.

Heat oil in skillet. Brown ham. Add onions, celery, and garlic, and sauté until caramelized.

Add thyme, oregano, and shrimp. Cook for about 10 minutes.

Add cheese, claw crabmeat, and eggplant. Add eggs, cayenne pepper, white pepper, salt, green onions, and ¾ cup breadcrumbs. Cook for 5 minutes.

Remove from heat. Fold in jumbo lump crabmeat. Place filling in an 8-cup baking dish. Top with breadcrumbs and dot with butter. Bake for 20-25 minutes at 350 degrees, until browned and bubbly.

Crab and Cauliflower au Gratin

Serves 4

Until the 1950s, the neighborhood butcher whose shop predated Manale's provided the very finest cuts of meat for the restaurant—making Manale's as famous for steaks as they were for seafood. In this dish, big lumps of crabmeat are stirred into a rich cauliflower au gratin, creating a perfect side for any juicy steak or chop.

1 cup cauliflower florets
6 tbsp. butter
6 tbsp. flour
1 cup milk
½ cup shredded cheddar cheese, plus 2 tbsp.
   for topping
1 lb. lump crabmeat
½ tsp. salt
¼ tsp. white pepper

Blanch cauliflower in salted boiling water until just tender. Drain and reserve.

In a saucepan over medium heat, whisk together butter and flour until flour is cooked (3-4 minutes). Whisk in milk and cook over medium low until thickened. Stir in cheddar cheese, mixing until smooth.

Gently fold in cauliflower and crabmeat. Season with salt and pepper. Divide into 4 au gratin dishes and top with additional cheddar cheese. Bake at 350 degrees for 25-30 minutes until browned and bubbly.

Crabmeat Verdi

Serves 4-6

Frances Radosta's love of opera is well documented, so it's no surprise that this Manale classic baked crabmeat dish was named for the beloved nineteenth-century operatic composer, Giuseppe Verdi.

¼ cup olive oil
3 garlic cloves, chopped
2 tbsp. chopped fresh parsley
½ cup white wine
½ cup plain breadcrumbs, plus 2 tbsp. for
    topping
1 lb. lump crabmeat

Mix all ingredients together. Spoon into a baking dish. Sprinkle the top with additional breadcrumbs. Bake in a preheated 350-degree oven for 15 minutes until browned. Serve at once.

Crawfish Etouffee

Serves 4-6

Etouffee is sometimes made with shrimp or chicken, but the best etouffee of the year is made in the springtime, with freshly caught crawfish, right out of Louisiana's rice fields.

12 oz. butter
3 garlic cloves, chopped
1 medium onion, chopped
1 green bell pepper, chopped
3 stalks celery, chopped
2 bay leaves
½ tsp. thyme
¼ tsp. oregano
½ cup flour
2 tsp. paprika
1 14.5-oz. can diced tomatoes
½ cup chicken stock
1 cup shrimp stock
¼ tsp. cayenne pepper
½ tsp. salt
2 tsp. Lea & Perrins Worcestershire sauce
½ tsp. hot sauce
6 green onions, sliced
1 lb. Louisiana crawfish tails
4 cups cooked rice

Heat butter in a saucepan over medium heat. Add garlic, onion, bell pepper, and celery. Sauté until tender.

Add bay leaves, thyme, and oregano. Whisk in flour to create a roux. Add paprika and tomatoes, stirring constantly over medium-high heat for 5 minutes.

Add both stocks and bring to a boil, then simmer for 30 minutes. Add cayenne, salt, Worcestershire, hot sauce, and green onions. Cook for 15 more minutes.

Add crawfish tails. Return to a simmer. Remove from heat. Serve over rice.

Championship golfer Jack Nicklaus (Photograph courtesy of DeFelice Family Collection)

Baked Italian Crawfish

Serves 4-6

The crawfish are distinctly Louisiana, but the seasonings are all Italian in this baked dish that can serve as an appetizer or entrée.

4 tbsp. olive oil
6 green onions, thinly sliced
2 garlic cloves, chopped
¼ tsp. thyme
⅛ tsp. oregano
¼ tsp. basil
¼ cup dry white wine
1 lb. crawfish tails
4 tbsp. grated Romano cheese
Salt, pepper, and hot sauce to taste
2 tsp. plain breadcrumbs
2 tbsp. butter

Preheat oven to 375 degrees. Heat olive oil in a skillet. Sauté green onions, garlic, thyme, oregano, and basil until soft.

Add white wine and bring to a boil. Remove from heat and stir in crawfish tails. Mix in cheese and season to taste with salt, pepper, and hot sauce.

Spoon mixture into a baking dish. Sprinkle top with breadcrumbs and dot with butter. Bake for 20-25 minutes until golden brown.

Crawfish and Andouille Pasta

Serves 6

Andouille sausage was not regularly seen on New Orleans menus until the 1980s, when Cajun ingredients became common in the city. The smoky sausage pairs beautifully with crawfish tails in this simple, creamy dish.

½ lb. andouille, chopped
1 tbsp. butter
1 red onion, chopped
4 garlic cloves, chopped
½ tsp. salt
1 tsp. crushed red pepper flakes
6 green onions, chopped
1 cup heavy cream
1 lb. crawfish tails
1 lb. penne pasta, cooked

In a skillet, render andouille in butter until andouille begins to brown. Add onion, garlic, salt, red pepper, and green onions. Sauté until softened.

Add heavy cream and cook on high until reduced and thickened. Stir in crawfish tails and heat through. Toss in penne pasta and serve.

Poisson Catherine

Serves 4

This fish dish is named for everyone's favorite waitress, Catherine Daniels, a fixture at Manale's for over fifty years.

4 trout (or other white fish) filets
¼ cup flour, lightly seasoned with salt and
  pepper
4 tbsp. butter
1 lemon, juiced
3 tbsp. capers, whole
2 tbsp. chopped fresh parsley
1 cup Manale Hollandaise Sauce (see index)

Lightly dredge each fillet in seasoned flour. Melt butter in a skillet. Brown filets on each side. Sprinkle with lemon juice.

Mix capers and parsley into hollandaise sauce. Top each filet with sauce and serve.

(Photograph by Sam Hanna)

Grilled Fish Orleans

Serves 4

Artichokes, mushrooms, and shrimp combine to make a light, elegant sauce for a piece of fresh Gulf fish.

2 tbsp. olive oil
1 lb. small raw shrimp, peeled and deveined
2 oz. brandy
3 green onions, chopped
4 tbsp. diced red bell pepper
3 garlic cloves, chopped
1 cup sliced fresh mushrooms
1 14.5-oz. can quartered artichoke hearts, drained
1 cup dry white wine
4 tbsp. cold butter, cubed and lightly tossed in flour
1 lb. spaghetti, cooked
4 fresh fish filets, 6-8 oz. each, grilled or sautéed
1 tsp. chopped fresh parsley

Heat olive oil in sauté pan. Add shrimp, and sauté until shrimp are just pink and firm. Remove shrimp from pan and reserve.

Add brandy and flambé. Add green onions, red peppers, garlic, and mushrooms, and sauté until soft. Add artichokes and white wine. Reduce liquid by half, then return shrimp to pan.

Whisk in butter to emulsify. Add spaghetti, and mix thoroughly. Plate fish and spaghetti side by side. Top fish filets with sauce, and garnish with chopped parsley.

Pan-Seared Catfish

Serves 4

While trout and red snapper dominated Manale's menus during much of the twentieth century, catfish is now a favorite of many regular diners.

4 6-oz. catfish filets
½ cup seasoned flour
4 tbsp. olive oil
¼ cup white wine
2 tbsp. lemon juice
¼ cup canned quartered artichoke hearts
4 tbsp. cold butter, cubed and lightly tossed in
    seasoned flour
1 lb. lump crabmeat
1 lb. spaghetti, cooked

Dredge catfish in seasoned flour. Heat olive oil in a skillet. Brown catfish on each side and reserve.

Deglaze pan with white wine and lemon juice. Bring to a boil and add artichoke hearts. Toss cold butter in seasoned flour. Whisk into pan juices.

Add crabmeat and mix well. Return catfish to the skillet and bring all to a boil. Serve catfish with spaghetti on the side, sauced with artichoke and crabmeat.

(Photograph by Sam Hanna)

Stuffed Shrimp

Serves 4

This dish features jumbo shrimp, stuffed with a big ball of crab and shrimp stuffing and fried to golden perfection.

12 large (16-20 per lb.) raw shrimp
1 cup cubed stale French bread
½ cup shrimp stock
3 tbsp. olive oil
2 garlic cloves, chopped
1 onion, chopped
3 stalks celery, chopped
½ green bell pepper, chopped
4 green onions, chopped
¼ tsp. thyme
⅛ tsp. oregano
⅛ tsp. sage
½ tsp. salt
¼ tsp. pepper
¼ lb. small (41-50 per lb.) raw shrimp, chopped
½ lb. claw crabmeat
4 eggs
3 tbsp. chopped fresh parsley
1 egg
1 cup milk
1 cup flour
1 cup corn flour
Vegetable oil for deep frying

Peel and butterfly the large shrimp, leaving the tails intact. Refrigerate until ready to use. Moisten French bread with shrimp stock and reserve.

Heat olive oil in a skillet. Sauté garlic, onion, celery, bell pepper, and green onions until softened. Sprinkle on thyme, oregano, sage, salt, and pepper and sauté for 1 minute.

Remove from heat and stir in chopped shrimp and claw crabmeat. Cool slightly. Beat 4 eggs together and add to the mixture, along with the moistened bread and chopped parsley.

Place each shrimp on a baking pan, flattened out. Scoop about 2-3 tbsp. stuffing on top of the shrimp and partially freeze (at least 30 minutes). When ready to prepare, beat together 1 egg and milk to make an egg wash.

Carefully roll each stuffed shrimp in flour, dip in egg wash, and roll in corn flour. Fry in 360-degree oil till lightly browned (about 4-5 minutes). Drain and serve.

NOTE: Partially freezing the stuffed shrimp makes them hold together well while frying. This is the Manale procedure, but you may fry them immediately without partially freezing them first. Stuffed shrimp will store well, frozen, for up to 6 months, before you flour and fry them.

Stuffed Crab

Yields 6 crabs

When Manale's was considered the Uptown spot for boiled seafood, a rich, crab stuffing was often heaped right into the original crimson shells and baked. In the twenty-first century, aluminum crab shells have taken the place of the authentic originals at the restaurant, but nothing has changed about the taste!

2 tbsp. olive oil
2 stalks celery, finely chopped
1 green bell pepper, finely chopped
1 onion, finely chopped
½ tsp. thyme
2 eggs, beaten
½ cup plain breadcrumbs, plus 2 tbsp. for
  topping
1 lb. claw crabmeat
½ tsp. salt
¼ tsp. pepper
6 cleaned crab shells

Heat olive oil in a skillet. Add celery, bell pepper, and onion. Sprinkle thyme over seasoning vegetables. Sauté until translucent. Remove from heat.

Stir in eggs and breadcrumbs. Fold in crabmeat. Season with salt and pepper. Spoon approximately ½ cup mixture into each crab shell or some substitute. Sprinkle breadcrumbs on top and bake in a preheated 325-degree oven for 25-30 minutes till browned.

Softshell Crab Pascal

Serves 4

4 softshell crabs
1 cup Barbeque Shrimp Sauce (see index)
1 lb. peeled small raw shrimp
1 egg
2 cups milk
1½ cups seasoned corn flour
Vegetable oil for frying

Clean the softshell crabs by using kitchen shears to remove the eyes and mouth from each crab. (Make sure to cut through the fluid-filled sac behind the face to prevent popping and splattering while frying.) Remove the flap from the underside of the crab. Lift up each pointed side of the top shell and remove the feathery gills, pulling them away from the body and snipping them off.

Heat the barbeque sauce over medium heat. Add the shrimp, cooking gently until the shrimp are firm and just cooked (5 minutes or less). Reserve the barbeque shrimp, keeping warm.

Mix together egg and milk to make an egg wash. Soak each crab in the egg wash before dredging in the corn flour. Heat the oil to 365 degrees. Fry the softshell crabs, turning once to brown on each side (about 4-5 minutes). Drain well. To serve, sauce each fried softshell crab with barbeque shrimp and ¼ cup sauce.

(Photograph by Sam Hanna)

food

food

very
Good

June

Chapter 7
Meat

Manale's Meatballs

Yields 6 5-oz. meatballs

For most of Manale's history, the meatballs were made daily by the ladies of the family. Pascal's sisters never married and lived with family all of their lives, so they rolled countless meatballs—always in two sizes, a gargantuan ball of almost a half-pound and also a smaller, more traditional sized meatball. Pascal's nephew Martin loved to be sent out for afternoon pickup. First, he'd pick up the night's hot, fresh French bread from Leidenheimer's and then, he'd head over to Louisiana Avenue Parkway for the meatballs and gravy. Needless to say, many a meatball sandwich was enjoyed en route back to restaurant.

6 cups cubed, dry French bread
1 cup milk
2 lb. ground beef
2 medium onions, chopped
8 garlic cloves, chopped
4 tbsp. chopped fresh parsley
1 tsp. salt
½ tsp. pepper
6 eggs
3 tbsp. Lea & Perrins Worcestershire sauce
1 tbsp. hot sauce
¾ cup breadcrumbs
½ cup grated Romano cheese

Soak French bread in milk for 5 minutes until softened. In a large bowl, mix together the ground beef, onions, garlic, and parsley. Sprinkle on salt and pepper, then mix in the raw eggs, Worcestershire, and hot sauce.

Add the softened French bread, and then tighten the mixture with dried breadcrumbs and Romano cheese. Form into balls and place on a heavy, rimmed baking pan. Bake at 300 degrees for 1 hour. Simmer meatballs in red gravy and serve with spaghetti.

(Photograph by Sam Hanna)

Daube

Serve 6

French daube is an entirely different dish from Sicilian-New Orleans daube. It's also drastically different from New Orleans' other daube, "daube glace," a jellied beef dish similar to hogshead cheese. The dish is said to have originated in Provence, where most households have a daubiere, a distinctive terracotta pot used for braising inexpensive cuts of beef. In New Orleans, the beef braises slowly in a red gravy redolent with red wine. Manale's daube is served with spaghetti, but I often serve mine with curly rotini, which holds the beefy sauce in its indentations. The hardboiled egg garnish is a distinctly Sicilian-New Orleans touch.

2-3 lb. beef round roast
12 garlic cloves
Salt and pepper to taste
2 tbsp. olive oil
1 cup red wine
6 cups Red Gravy (see index)
1 lb. spaghetti, cooked
3 hardboiled eggs

Cut small slits into the roast, and insert the whole garlic cloves. Sprinkle liberally with salt and pepper. Heat olive oil in a heavy 5-qt. Dutch oven. Brown the roast on all sides. Remove from the pot.

Deglaze the pot with the red wine. Add the red gravy and return the roast to the pot. Cover tightly with aluminum foil, then cover with pot lid.

Place roast in a 325-degree oven and bake slowly for 1½ hours. Cool and slice roast, adding slices back into red gravy. Simmer on top of the stove until the meat begins to fall apart. Serve with spaghetti. Top each serving with a half of a hardboiled egg as garnish.

Brisket Marinara

Serves 6

New Orleans' "boiled beef" is a ubiquitous dish in traditional New Orleans restaurants. The cut of beef in question is always brisket, which becomes tender during long, vigorous simmering. Usually served with a spicy cocktail sauce and boiled potatoes, at Manale's it's sauced with marinara and accompanied by spaghetti or boiled potatoes.

3½-4 lb. brisket, trimmed
1 tsp. salt
½ tsp. pepper
2 gal. water
4 cups Marinara Sauce (see index)

Season the brisket with salt and pepper. Put the brisket, fat cap side down, in a large hot stockpot. When fat is rendered, brown brisket on other side. Drain off excess fat.

Cover the brisket with water. Bring to a boil, and then reduce to a simmer. Cook for 45 minutes to 1 hour, until tender. Drain, reserving beef stock for later use. Chill brisket for several hours or overnight.

Remove congealed fat from brisket and discard fat. Slice brisket thinly. Heat marinara sauce in a saucepan. Add 3-4 slices of brisket per person and simmer in marinara sauce for 15-20 minutes till heated through. Serve with boiled potatoes or spaghetti.

Ossobuco

Serves 4

Ossobuco translates from Italian as "bone with a hole," referring to the marrow hole at the center of cross-cut veal shanks. This classic is a newer offering at traditionally Sicilian style Manale's, as it hails from Milan, in Northern Italy.

4 12-14-oz. veal shanks (center cut)
Salt and white pepper to taste
4 tbsp. flour
2 tbsp. olive oil
½ cup red wine
1 green bell pepper, chopped
½ onion, chopped
4 stalks celery, chopped
8 garlic cloves, chopped
2 tbsp. tomato puree
2 cups beef stock
2 bay leaves
½ tsp. thyme
Zest of 1 lemon
1 orange, zested and juiced
1 onion, julienned
1 red bell pepper, julienned
1 green bell pepper, julienned
2 stalks celery, julienned
4 carrots, peeled and julienned

Salt and pepper shanks. Lightly flour shanks. Heat oil in an 7-qt. sauteuse pan. Brown shanks on both sides. Remove shanks from pan.

Deglaze pan with red wine. Add bell pepper, onion, celery, and garlic and sauté over for 10 minutes. Add tomato puree and sauté for 2-3 minutes.

Add beef stock, bay leaves, thyme, zest of lemon, and zest and juice of orange. Bring to a boil and reduce by half. Strain reduced sauce through chinoise.

Put strained sauce and shanks back into pot. Simmer for 1 hour until shanks are tender. Add julienned vegetables to sauce and simmer till tender. Serve with rice or pasta.

Mark and Rachel DeFelice (Photograph by Sam Hanna)

Veal Chop with Portobello Mushroom Demi-Glace

Serves 4

Rachel DeFelice coaxed her dad, Mark, into allowing her to experiment at Manale's with dishes she'd learned to cook while apprenticing in Europe. The risotto she mastered there adds an opulent touch to a succulent veal chop sauced with demi-glace.

4 12-14-oz. bone-in veal chops
¼ cup port wine
4 portobello mushrooms, sliced ¼ inch thick
2 cups veal demi-glace
Rachel's Risotto (see index)

In a heavy skillet, cook chops to desired doneness. Remove from skillet. Deglaze the skillet with port wine and add the mushrooms. When the mushrooms begin to cook, add the veal demi-glace and bring to a simmer. Return chops to the skillet and turn once to coat both sides. Sauce chops with mushroom demi-glace and serve with Rachel's Risotto.

(Photograph by Sam Hanna)

Veal Bracioloni

Serves 4

At one time, this dish could be found on every New Orleans Italian restaurant menu and in every Sicilian-New Orleans home. There are almost as many variations of the dish as there are cooks; some include spinach or carrots, some include prosciutto and provolone. In Sicily, raisins and pine nuts are often found in the stuffing, something rarely seen in New Orleans versions.

1 lb. ground veal
3 garlic cloves, finely chopped
1 stalk celery, finely chopped
4 tbsp. finely chopped green bell pepper
½ onion, finely chopped
1 tbsp. chopped fresh parsley
4 hardboiled eggs, chopped
½ cup breadcrumbs
1 egg, beaten
½ tsp. salt
¼ tsp. pepper
8 veal scallops, pounded thin
Salt and pepper to taste
2 tbsp. olive oil
2½ cups Red Gravy (see index)

(Photograph by Sam Hanna)

In a heavy skillet, brown the ground veal. Add the garlic, celery, bell pepper, and onion. Sauté until seasoning vegetables are translucent. Remove from heat.

Stir in parsley and hardboiled eggs. Add breadcrumbs to tighten up the mixture. Mix in beaten egg. Season with ½ tsp. salt and ¼ tsp. pepper.

Place a couple of tablespoons of stuffing into the center of each veal scallop, roll up scallop, and fasten with toothpicks. Season lightly with salt and pepper. Heat olive oil and brown each of the stuffed rolls on both sides.

Add the red gravy to the pan, cover tightly, and bake for 25-30 minutes in a 325-degree oven. Carefully remove all toothpicks before serving. Serve with spaghetti, sauced with red gravy.

Veal Marsala

Serves 4

Marsala wine is a Sicilian fortified wine much like port, madeira, and sherry. Marsala as a dish is of American invention, where garlic, mushrooms, and butter combine with the wine to make a rich, slightly sweet sauce for veal or chicken.

1 lb. veal scallops
½ cup flour
2 tbsp. olive oil
2 tbsp. butter
½ lb. mushrooms, sliced
2 garlic cloves, chopped
½ cup marsala wine
¾ cup beef stock
Salt and pepper to taste

Lightly dust veal with flour. Heat olive oil in a skillet and sauté veal on each side until browned. Remove from pan and reserve.

Add butter to skillet along with mushrooms and garlic. Sauté together briefly, then add marsala wine. Bring to a boil and add beef stock. Season with salt and pepper. Cook until mushrooms are tender. Return the veal to the pan and heat thoroughly. Serve with angel-hair pasta, turned in the sauce before serving.

(Photograph by Sam Hanna)

Veal Puccini

Serves 4

La Boheme, Tosca, and Madame Butterfly are just three of Giacomo Puccini's masterworks. Similar to a classic piccata, this delightful, light, lemony dish was honored with Puccini's name by Frances Radosta.

8 tbsp. butter
4 veal scallops, lightly dusted with flour
1 lb. mushrooms, thinly sliced
2 tbsp. flour
¼ cup white wine
½ cup chicken stock
1 tbsp. lemon juice
¼ tsp. salt
⅛ tsp. white pepper
1 lb. spaghetti, cooked

Melt 2 tbsp. butter in a skillet. Sauté the veal till lightly browned on both sides. Remove from pan and reserve.

Add the mushrooms and sauté for 2 minutes, then reserve. Add 2 tbsp. butter to the skillet and melt. Whisk in flour, whisking over medium heat for 2-3 minutes until flour is cooked but does not change color.

Whisk in white wine, chicken stock, and lemon juice. Add salt and white pepper. Bring to a simmer. Return veal and mushrooms to the skillet and whisk in the last of the butter. Roll spaghetti in the butter sauce, and top with veal scallops and additional sauce.

Veal Piccata

Serves 4

Lemon juice and capers provide a piquant accent to the rich, buttery sauce.

8 3-oz. veal rounds, thinly sliced
¼ cup seasoned flour
2 tbsp. olive oil
1 cup white wine
3 tbsp. lemon juice
2 tbsp. capers
Salt and white pepper to taste
2 tbsp. cold butter, cut in pieces and lightly
    tossed in seasoned flour
1 lb. spaghetti, cooked

Dredge each piece of veal in seasoned flour. Heat olive oil in skillet, and sauté veal till lightly browned on each side. Remove from skillet and reserve.

Add white wine and lemon juice, and deglaze skillet. Add capers, salt, and white pepper. Return veal to skillet.

Whisk cold, seasoned butter into the sauce to thicken. Turn cooked spaghetti in sauce. Serve veal on top of rolled spaghetti, with extra caper sauce on top.

(Photograph by Sam Hanna)

Chicken and Crab Napoleon

Serves 4

Named for the avenue on which Manale's sits, the combination of fresh Gulf crabmeat and mozzarella cheese stuffed into chicken breasts makes for an elegant, delectable dish—especially when topped with rich Scarpia sauce.

1 egg
½ cup milk
4 boneless chicken breasts
½ tsp. salt
¼ tsp. white pepper
¼ tsp. thyme
½ cup shredded mozzarella cheese
½ lb. jumbo lump crabmeat
2 cups plain breadcrumbs
Vegetable oil for deep frying
2 cups Scarpia sauce (see index for Shrimp a la
    Scarpia)

Mix together egg and milk to make egg wash and reserve. Pound each chicken breast into an even thickness of ¼ inch. Mix seasonings together and lightly season each breast on both sides.

In the center of each breast, place a small amount of cheese, topped with crabmeat. Tightly roll each breast around cheese and crabmeat. Dip each breast in egg wash, then roll in breadcrumbs, and fry until browned on both sides. Serve topped with Scarpia sauce, alongside spaghetti.

NOTE: The chicken breasts can be oven baked instead of fried.

Chicken Alfredo

Serves 4

The original Alfredo sauce, said to have been invented in Rome by Alfredo Di Lelio in 1892, was a simple combination of butter and cheese. The Manale's rich, creamy version is brightened by the addition of fresh lemon juice.

4 6-oz. boneless, skinless chicken breasts
¼ tsp. salt
¼ tsp. white pepper
2 tbsp. olive oil
5 garlic cloves, chopped
2 lemons, juiced
½ cup white wine
2 cups heavy cream
¼ cup chicken stock
6 oz. fettuccine, cooked
2 oz. grated Romano cheese
Salt and white pepper to taste

Tenderize chicken with mallet. Season chicken with ¼ tsp. salt and ¼ tsp. white pepper. Heat olive oil in a skillet and brown chicken on both sides.

In a saucepan, combine garlic, lemon juice, and white wine. Reduce by two-thirds. Add cream, whisking constantly until cream reduces by half.

Heat chicken stock in a skillet. Toss in fettuccine and Romano cheese. Slice chicken breasts into strips, combine with cream sauce, and toss into pasta. Season to taste with salt and white pepper and serve.

(Photograph by Sam Hanna)

Chicken Cacciatore

Serves 4-6

Cacciatore means "hunter" in Italian. The Manale's version of this classic dish veers far from the ordinary with the addition of kalamata olives and green peas. Using creole sauce instead of the usual marinara makes for a distinctly New Orleans style dish.

1 whole chicken, cut into pieces
½ cup flour lightly seasoned with salt and
    pepper
¼ cup olive oil
4 cups Creole Sauce (see index)
1 cup green peas, frozen or canned
¼ cup halved kalamata olives
½ tsp. salt
¼ tsp. white pepper
1 lb. spaghetti, cooked

Dust the chicken pieces with seasoned flour. Heat olive oil in a heavy sauteuse pan, and brown chicken pieces on both sides. Remove chicken and reserve.

Add creole sauce to sauteuse pan and bring to a simmer. Return chicken to sauce and add green peas and kalamata olives. Reduce heat to low and cook until chicken is tender. Season with salt and pepper. Serve with spaghetti.

Chicken Bordelaise

Serves 4

The French red-wine sauce with butter and delicate shallots known as Bordelaise bears little resemblance to the New Orleans version, which is redolent with garlic tempered by chopped fresh parsley. Often served to accompany steaks, at Manale's chicken and pasta provide the perfect foil for the garlicky sauce.

4 chicken breasts, pounded ¼ inch thin
Seasoned flour for dredging
4 tbsp. butter, melted
1 lb. mushrooms, sliced
2 garlic cloves, chopped
1½ tbsp. chopped fresh parsley
1 cup white wine
½ cup veal or chicken stock
4 tbsp. cold butter, cut into chunks
1 lb. pasta, cooked

Lightly dredge the chicken breasts in flour and sauté in melted butter till browned on both sides. Remove and reserve. Add mushrooms to pan and sauté for 3-4 minutes.

Add garlic and parsley and sauté together for 1 minute, then add white wine and stock. Bring all to a boil. Return chicken breasts to sauce and simmer for 3-4 minutes.

Toss cold butter chunks in dredging flour, lightly coating them. Whisk coated butter into the sauce to thicken. Turn hot pasta in the sauce, then plate. Top pasta with chicken breasts and remaining sauce.

Dining room, 1940s (Photograph courtesy of Radosta Family Collection)

Rosemary Chicken

Serves 4

Combining the techniques of roasting and braising, this simple dish is satisfyingly redolent of rosemary and garlic.

1 whole chicken, cut into pieces
½ cup seasoned flour for dredging
¼ cup olive oil
1 cup white wine
18-24 whole garlic cloves
2 tbsp. rosemary leaves
½ tsp. salt
¼ tsp. white pepper
2 tbsp. butter, cut into chunks

Lightly toss chicken in seasoned flour, shaking off any excess. Heat the olive oil in a large, deep sauteuse pan. Brown the chicken pieces on all sides. Remove chicken and reserve.

Add the white wine and deglaze the pan. Add garlic cloves, rosemary, salt, and pepper. Return chicken to the pan and turn, coating with the sauce. Cover the pan tightly and bake at 375 degrees for 20 minutes, then increase the temperature to 425 degrees and roast lightly for 5 minutes. Remove chicken from pan and whisk in butter to thicken sauce. Spoon thickened sauce over chicken and serve immediately with potatoes or pasta.

(Photograph by Sam Hanna)

Red Beans

Serves 6-8

Red beans and rice are a Monday tradition in New Orleans, both at home and in restaurants across the city. The Manale's version utilizes the flavor bomb of ground bacon and red and green bell peppers.

1 lb. dried red beans
½ lb. bacon, finely ground
½ red bell pepper, chopped
½ green bell pepper, chopped
4 garlic cloves, chopped
1 onion, chopped
2 stalks celery, chopped
1 qt. water
3 bay leaves
1 tbsp. salt
1 tsp. pepper
Cooked rice

Soak beans for 2½ hours or overnight. Drain beans. In a heavy 5-qt. saucepan, sauté bacon until it has cooked through and rendered its fat.

Add bell peppers, garlic, onion, and celery. Sauté for another 5 minutes until the vegetables are translucent. Add beans and cover with water. Bring to a boil.

Add bay leaves, salt, and pepper. Reduce to a simmer. Cook for 2-3 hours, stirring frequently until thick and creamy. Add more liquid if necessary. Serve over rice.

Liver and Onions

Serves 4

In the early days, Manale's served breakfast along with its full menu of Italian specialties and seafood. Guests could choose from fifteen varieties of omelettes or order eggs boiled, scrambled, poached, or shirred. Their version of New Orleans' classic breakfast, liver and onions, was topped with crisp bacon strips and a sunny-side-up egg.

12 slices bacon
1 onion, thinly sliced
1 lb. calf's liver, thinly sliced
¼ cup seasoned flour for dredging
4 tbsp. flour
2 tbsp. vegetable oil
1 cup beef stock
Salt and pepper to taste
2 cups Creamy Manale's Grits (see index)
4 fried eggs

In a large, heavy skillet, fry bacon and reserve. Add onions to the bacon drippings and sauté until golden brown. Remove and reserve.

Lightly dust the calf's liver with seasoned flour. Brown in oil on each side and remove from pan. Sprinkle 4 tbsp. flour over the pan and cook over medium heat, scraping up bits as they stick.

Add beef stock to the skillet and scrape the bottom to deglaze the pan thoroughly. Return liver and onions to the pan and simmer together for 5 minutes. Season with salt and pepper. Serve liver on grits, topped with onions, bacon slices, and a fried egg.

(Photograph by Sam Hanna)

RELISHES, ETC.

Celery	.20
Queen, Ripe or Stuffed Olives	.20
Sour Pickles	.10
Dill Pickles	.15
Sweet Pickles	.25
Imported Anchovies	.50
Imported Anti Pasto	.50
Sardines (per can)	.40
Iced River Shrimp	.40
Iced Lake Shrimp	.35
Grape Fruit, half	.15
Shrimp Cocktail	.25
Crab Meat Cocktail	.30
Crayfish	
Celery, Stuffed with Roquefort Cheese	.50

SOUPS

Oyster	.25
Chicken Broth	.25
Ox Tail	.25
Cream of Tomato	.25
Vegetable	.25
Turtle	.25
Tomato	.25
Creole Gumbo	.25
Cream of Celery	.25
Mushroom	.25

FISH, OYSTERS, ETC.

Oyster Cocktail	.20	.40
Oysters, Stewed	.25	.40
Oysters, Fried	.30	.60
Oysters en Brochette	.40	.75
Oysters, Broiled on Toast	.40	.75
Oysters, Shell Roast	.40	.75
Oysters, Pan Roast	.40	.75
Soft Shell Crabs		.65
Tenderloin of Trout, Tartar Sauce		.50
Spanish Mackerel		.60
Frog Legs		.75
Frog Legs Saute with Mushrooms		1.00
Stuffed Crabs (1)		.15

SALADS, ETC.

Special Salad	.35
Lettuce	.15
Tomato	.15
Lettuce and Tomato	.20
Combination	.25
Potato	.15
Tomato and Onion	.20
Shrimp Mayonnaise	.40
Chicken Mayonnaise	.40
Asparagus Vinaigrette	.40
Alligator Pear, Half	

OUR SPECIALTY

Half Spring Chicken with Spaghetti	1.00
Daube with Spaghetti	.80
Meat Balls with Spaghetti	.75
Spaghetti with Green Peas	.70
Spaghetti Italian	.50
Spaghetti a la Manale	.60
Welsh Rarebit	.50
Golden Buck	.60
Cold Sliced Chicken	.75
Assorted Cold Meats, Potato Salad	.50
Chicken a la King	1.00

DISHES TO ORDER

STEAKS—

Sirloin Steak	1.00
Sirloin, Smothered with Onions	1.35
Sirloin, Smothered with Mushrooms	1.40
Sirloin a la Creole	1.35

CHOPS—

Lamb Chops (2)	.50
Pork Chops (2)	.50
Veal Chops (2)	.50
Veal Chops, Breaded (2)	.50

CHICKEN—

Half Spring Chicken, Broiled or Fried	.65
Half Spring Chicken, Country Style	.90
Half Spring Chicken a la Creole	1.15
Half Spring Chicken with Mushrooms	1.25
Half Spring Chicken with Green Peas	1.15
Chicken Liver Omelette	.50
Broiled Chicken Liver	.60

SANDWICHES

Soft Shell Crab Sandwich	.35
Oyster Sandwich	.20
Ham, Broiled on Toast	.20
Ham, Boiled	.15
Chicken	.30
Club	.50
Sardine	.20
Swiss Cheese	.15
American Cheese	.15
Tongue	.15
Combination Ham and Cheese	.25
Ham and Egg Sandwich	.30
Gold Brick	.30
Special Roast Beef	.25
Dantonia Special	.40
Hamburger	.20
Hot Roast Beef	.25

Manale's menu from the 1930s (Photograph courtesy of Radosta Family Collection)

SPECIALS

Soft Shell Crabs, Julienne Potatoes, Tartar Sauce	.65
Shrimp a la Creole with Rice	.50
Fried Frog Legs, Julienne Potatoes, Tartar Sauce	.75
Broiled Speckled Trout, Tartar Sauce	.60
Fried Speckled Trout, Tartar Sauce	.50
Broiled Tenderloin of Trout, Tartar Sauce	.60
Fried Tenderloin of Trout, Tartar Sauce	.50
Half Broiled or Fried Spring Chicken and Potatoes	.65
Spaghetti and Ravioli .90 — Chicken a la King	1.00
Assorted Cold Meats and Potato Salad .50; with Chicken	.75
Tomato Stuffed with Chicken or Shrimp	.40
Cold Sliced Chicken with Tomato	.75
Crayfish Bisque	.30

VEGETABLES

Potatoes, French Fried	.15
Potatoes, Julienne	.15
Potatoes, Saratoga Chips	.15
Potatoes, German Fried	.20
Potatoes, Hashed Browned	.20
Potatoes, Brabant	.20
Potatoes, Au Gratin	.25
Potatoes, Mashed	.15
Potatoes, Hashed in Cream	.25
Potatoes, O'Brien Au Gratin	.30
Potatoes, O'Brien Hashed Brown	.25
Green Peas	.20
Asparagus, Hot, Drawn Butter	.40
Asparagus, Cold, Vinagrette	.40
Spinach	.15
String Beans	.20

DESSERTS, CHEESE, ETC.

Roquefort Cheese and Jelly	.35
Swiss Cheese and Jelly	.25
American Cheese and Jelly	.25
Ice Cream, Vanilla	.15
Ice Cream, Chocolate or Tutti Fruitti	.15
Grape Fruit, Half	.15
Canteloupe, Half	.15
Watermelon	
Assorted Cakes	.10

BEERS

Dixie Draught, per Stein	.10
Dixie, Bottle	.15
Budweiser, Bottle	.20
Pabst, Bottle	.20
Bass Ale	.30
Ginn Stout	.30

EGGS, ETC.

Eggs, Boiled (2)	.25
Eggs, Scrambled (2)	.25
Eggs, Poached on Toast	.30
Eggs, Shirred (2)	.30
Ham and Eggs	.40
Bacon and Eggs	.40

OMELETTES

Plain	.25
Onion	.35
Parsley	.35
Oyster	.40
Jelly	.40
Cheese	.40
Ham	.40
Crab Meat	.50
A la Creole	.50
Asparagus	.45
Green Pea	.40
Bacon	.40
Spanish	.50
Mushroom	.60
Chicken Liver	.50

COFFEE, TEA, ETC.

Coffee	.05
Coffee, with Cream	.10
Tea	.10
Tea, per pot	.20
Tea, Iced	.10
Hot Chocolate	.10
Milk	.10
Toast	.10
Toasted Crackers	.10
Orange Marmalade	.25
Sliced Cake	.10
Pies, Apple, Lemon, Peach, per cut	.10

food

Chapter 8
Spaghetti and Sides

Spaghetti Collins

Serves 4

Named for New Orleans architect Collins Diboll, this simple dish of spaghetti can accompany any meat or fish.

1½ tbsp. olive oil
8 green onions, chopped
4 garlic cloves, chopped
¼ cup white wine
½ cup veal or chicken stock
2 tbsp. cold butter, cubed
½ tsp. salt
¼ tsp. white pepper
1 lb. spaghetti, cooked

Heat the olive oil in a skillet. Add the green onions and garlic. Sauté for 1 minute, then add white wine and stock.

Bring all to a boil. Boil for 3 minutes, then whisk in the butter to thicken the sauce. Season with salt and pepper. Twirl spaghetti in pan and then onto plate, adding more sauce as desired.

(Photograph by Sam Hanna)

Spaghetti Bordelaise

Serves 4

In New Orleans, many a newcomer is surprised to learn that our bordelaise bears little relation to the original, rich, red-wine sauce from Bordeaux. Manale's uses white wine instead, and the same sauce is also used to top chicken breasts.

1½ tbsp. olive oil
4 garlic cloves, chopped
6 tbsp. chopped fresh parsley
¼ cup white wine
½ cup veal or chicken stock
2 tbsp. butter
½ tsp. salt
¼ tsp. white pepper
1 lb. spaghetti, cooked

Heat the olive oil in a skillet. Add the garlic and parsley. Sauté for 1 minute, then add white wine and stock.

Bring all to a boil. Boil for 3 minutes, then whisk in the butter to thicken the sauce. Season with salt and pepper. Twirl spaghetti in pan and then onto plate, adding more sauce as desired.

Shrimp and Penne Pasta

Serves 4

Cylindrical, pen-shaped penne pasta is made both with and without tiny ridges. You'll want to use the ridged version in this dish, in order to trap every drop of the rich shrimp sauce.

2 lb. shrimp, peeled and deveined
6 tbsp. olive oil
2 garlic cloves, chopped
1 fresh tomato, skinned, seeded, and diced
4 tbsp. diced roasted red peppers
1 red onion, chopped
6 basil leaves, sliced into a thin chiffonade
4 oz. brandy
¼ tsp. salt
⅛ tsp. white pepper
2 tbsp. crushed red pepper flakes
1 cup shrimp stock
3 tbsp. cold butter, lightly tossed in flour
1 lb. penne pasta, cooked
4 tbsp. grated Romano cheese
1 tsp. chopped fresh parsley

Sauté shrimp in olive oil over high heat for 2-3 minutes. Add garlic, tomato, red onion, red peppers, and basil. Cook together for 2-3 minutes.

Add brandy and flambé. Add salt, pepper, red pepper flakes, and stock. Let simmer for 3-4 minutes.

Whisk in butter to emulsify sauce. Toss in penne pasta and Romano cheese. Serve garnished with parsley.

(Photograph by Sam Hanna)

Prosciutto, Peppers, and Shrimp with Bowtie Pasta

Serves 4

Smoky prosciutto and sweet peppers are perfect complements to fresh Gulf shrimp, with bowtie pasta adding a whimsical, toothsome touch.

2 tbsp. olive oil
8 slices prosciutto, cut into strips
1 lb. small peeled raw shrimp
2 tbsp. diced roasted red peppers
4 garlic cloves, chopped
6 green onion, chopped
4 tbsp. vodka
½ cup shrimp stock
4 tbsp. unsalted butter, cubed and floured
Salt, white pepper, and crushed red pepper
  flakes to taste
1 tbsp. chopped fresh parsley
1 lb. bowtie pasta, cooked

Heat olive oil in sauté pan. Add prosciutto and cook until crisp. Add shrimp and sauté for 1-2 minutes.

Add red peppers, garlic, and green onion. Deglaze pan with vodka. Add stock and bring to a simmer.

Whisk in butter and season to taste. Add parsley. Toss pasta in sauce and serve.

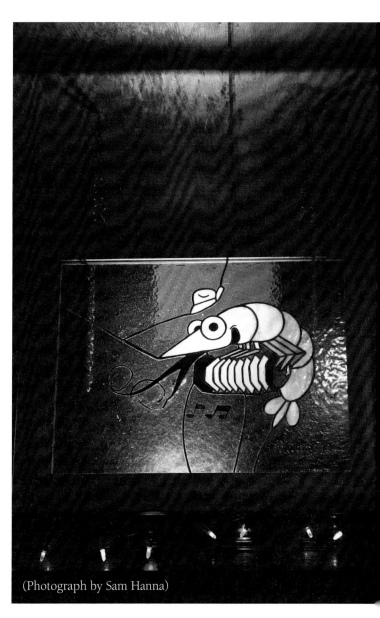

(Photograph by Sam Hanna)

Stuffed Tufoli

Serves 6

Tufoli is another special family recipe that was prepared in the Radosta home, then delivered to the restaurant, as were the meatballs and stuffed artichokes. Tufoli noodles are described as large, tubular pasta with a slight curve, but cannelloni noodles are the best substitute for the now elusive tufoli. The filling is also delicious for stuffing large shell pasta.

1 lb. ground veal or beef
4 garlic cloves, chopped
1 medium onion, chopped
½ medium green bell pepper, chopped
2 stalks celery, chopped
1 tsp. thyme
¼ tsp. oregano
8 oz. frozen chopped spinach, defrosted and
    squeezed dry
½ tsp. salt
¼ tsp. white pepper
1 egg
3 hardboiled eggs, chopped
¼ cup grated Romano cheese
12 tufoli or cannelloni noodles, cooked till just
    al dente
1½ cups Red Gravy (see index)
½ cup shredded mozzarella cheese

In heavy skillet, brown meat, then add garlic, onion, bell pepper, and celery. Sauté together until seasoning vegetables are translucent. Sprinkle on thyme and oregano.

Stir in spinach. Season mixture with salt and pepper, and then add egg, mixing well. Stir in hardboiled eggs and Romano cheese.

Spoon mixture into a pastry bag and fill each pasta tube. Spoon half of red gravy into a casserole dish, spreading to coat the bottom. Add the tufoli, topped with remaining red gravy and finished with mozzarella cheese. Bake in a 325-degree oven for 35-40 minutes until bubbly.

(Photographs by Sam Hanna)

Baked Lasagna

Serves 8

Manale's lasagna stands out from the rest with a layer of meaty eggplant rounds.
The hardboiled eggs are a distinctly Sicilian-New Orleans touch.

¼ cup olive oil
1 onion, chopped
3 stalks celery, chopped
1 green bell pepper, chopped
3 garlic cloves, chopped
1¾ lb. ground beef
2 cups sliced mushrooms
Salt and pepper to taste
¼ tsp. hot sauce
2 tbsp. Lea & Perrins Worcestershire sauce
4 cups Red Gravy (see index)
4 tbsp. chopped fresh parsley
1 cup ricotta cheese
½ lb. lasagna noodles, cooked
12 fried or roasted eggplant rounds
2 hardboiled eggs, sliced
1 cup grated mozzarella cheese
½ cup grated Romano cheese

Heat olive oil in a 5-qt. saucepot over medium heat. Add onion, celery, bell pepper, and garlic. Sauté until soft.

In a skillet, sauté the ground beef and mushrooms until browned. Add salt, pepper, hot sauce, and Worcestershire. Add to the saucepot with the red gravy. Simmer together for 30 minutes.

Mix together the parsley and ricotta cheese. Spread ¼ cup meat sauce on the bottom of a 9x13-inch baking pan. Take half of the lasagna noodles and add to the pan in a layer. Top with the eggplant, one-third of the remaining meat sauce, the sliced hardboiled eggs, ricotta, mozzarella, and Romano cheeses.

Top with half the remaining meat sauce and bake in a preheated 325-degree oven for 20 minutes. Add a final layer of lasagna noodles topped with the last of the meat sauce. Cover with aluminum foil and bake for another 30 minutes.

Cavatelli Chicken Eggplant Francesca

Serves 4

Cavatelli pasta is made from an eggless semolina dough. With a shape reminiscent of tiny hot-dog buns, they have little hollows in the center and slight ridges that the Francesca Sauce clings to.

½ cup flour
¼ tsp. salt
¼ tsp. pepper
4 chicken breasts, slightly flattened
¼-½ cup olive oil
6 slices eggplant, ½ inch thick
1 cup sliced mushrooms
3 cups Francesca Sauce (recipe follows)
1 lb. cavatelli pasta, cooked
1 cup shredded mozzarella cheese

Combine flour with salt and pepper. Dredge chicken in seasoned flour. Heat ¼ cup olive oil in a skillet and sauté breasts on each side till lightly browned. Remove from pan.

Add more olive oil if needed and sauté eggplant until tender and lightly browned on each side. Remove and reserve. Add more olive oil if needed and sauté mushrooms, carefully scraping up all the bits from the bottom of the skillet.

Add Francesca Sauce to the mushrooms and bring to a simmer. Toss the cooked cavatelli lightly in ¼ cup Francesca Sauce. Pour the sauced cavatelli into a greased 10x12-inch casserole pan.

Top the cavatelli with the chicken breasts, then the eggplant slices. Cover with the remainder of the sauce, then sprinkle with mozzarella cheese. Bake for 15-20 minutes at 375 degrees until bubbly.

Francesca Sauce

Yields 3 cups

¼ cup olive oil
1 onion, chopped
1 green bell pepper, chopped
6 green onions, chopped
3 garlic cloves, chopped
1 12-oz. can tomato puree
1 bay leaf
1 cup sherry
Salt and pepper to taste

Heat olive oil in a saucepan. Add onion, bell pepper, green onions, and garlic. Sauté until translucent.

Add tomato puree and the bay leaf. Bring to a simmer and cook covered for 3 minutes. Add sherry and salt and pepper. Simmer another 3 minutes.

(Photograph courtesy of Radosta Family Collection)

Rachel's Risotto

Serves 4

Rachel DeFelice learned the fine points of making an authentic risotto during her apprenticeship in Europe.

4 cups veal stock
1 tbsp. saffron threads
2 tbsp. olive oil
1 onion, chopped
1 cup Arborio rice
¼ cup dry white wine
1 bay leaf
¼ cup grated Romano cheese
4 tbsp. unsalted butter
¼ tsp. salt
⅛ tsp. pepper

In a small saucepan over medium heat, bring the stock to a simmer, then stir in saffron and reserve over low heat. In a 2½-qt. saucepan, heat olive oil over medium heat. Add the onions and sauté until translucent.

Add the rice and stir until fully coated with the oil and lightly toasted but not browned. Add the wine and bay leaf, stirring constantly until the wine is fully absorbed. Add a ladle of the simmering stock and continue to cook, stirring constantly until the stock is fully absorbed.

Reduce heat to medium low and continue to add stock, in 4-oz. increments, stirring until each addition is absorbed. When the grains of rice are "al dente" (slightly firm to the bite but not crunchy), the risotto is done. Remove bay leaf, then stir in Romano cheese and butter. Season with salt and pepper and serve immediately.

Dirty Rice

Serves 6-8

Dark-brown gizzards and livers provide the "dirt" in New Orleans-style dirty rice. This meaty, rich, satisfying dish could almost serve as an entrée but is most often an accompaniment to chicken.

½ lb. chicken gizzards
5 cups water
½ tsp. salt
2 tbsp. vegetable oil
½ lb. chicken livers, chopped
1 onion, chopped
3 stalks celery, chopped
1 green bell pepper, chopped
6 green onions, chopped
3 garlic cloves, chopped
3 tbsp. chopped fresh parsley
2 cups raw white rice
Salt and pepper to taste

Boil the chicken gizzards in the water and salt until tender. Reserve gizzard stock. Finely chop gizzards in a food processor.

Heat oil in a 5-qt. saucepan. Sauté livers and gizzards until browned. Add seasoning vegetables and sauté until tender.

Stir in rice, sautéing until rice is milky colored. Add 4 cups gizzard stock, salt, and pepper. Bring to a boil, then reduce to a simmer.

Simmer, uncovered, without stirring for 20 minutes. Fluff up grains of rice with a fork. Adjust seasonings and serve.

Brabant Potatoes

Serves 6

These crispy, cubed potatoes are a popular New Orleans side dish.

½ cup vegetable oil
3 large Idaho potatoes, peeled and cut into
   1-inch cubes
Salt to taste

Heat the oil to 360 degrees in a large frying pan.
Add potatoes and cook until browned all over,
about 5-7 minutes. Season with salt and serve.

Garlic Mashed Potatoes

Serves 4

Just a touch of garlic adds an Italian accent to simple mashed potatoes.

4 large Idaho potatoes, peeled and diced
2½ cups water
4 oz. chopped garlic
1 stick butter
Salt and pepper to taste

Combine potatoes, water, garlic, and butter in saucepan. Cook over medium heat until potatoes become soft, stirring occasionally. Remove from heat and whisk until desired consistency. Season with salt and pepper.

(Photograph by Sam Hanna)

Creamy Manale's Grits

Serves 4

Milk or cream is often used to cook hominy grits, but only at Manale's will you find the accents of green onions and imported Romano cheese. These grits provide the perfect foil for buttery shrimp and beefy gravy alike.

2 cups water
1 cup heavy cream
½ tsp. salt
1½ cups white grits
6 tbsp. butter
4 green onions, thinly sliced
¼ cup grated Romano cheese

Bring water, cream, and salt to a boil in a 3-qt. saucepan. Whisk in the grits. Reduce to a simmer, cover, and cook, stirring every 5 minutes for 10-15 minutes. When grits are cooked, stir in butter, green onions, and cheese. Mix thoroughly.

Sautéed Spinach

Serves 4

Redolent with garlic and enriched with beef stock, Manale's sautéed spinach makes a perfect accompaniment to steaks and chops.

1 tbsp. olive oil
4 garlic cloves, chopped
⅛ cup white wine
¼ cup beef stock
Salt and pepper to taste
1 lb. fresh spinach

In a large skillet, heat olive oil. Add garlic and sauté for a few seconds, then add white wine, stock, salt, and pepper. Bring to a boil. Reduce by one-third, then add fresh spinach, turning in the pan until just wilted. Serve immediately.

Creamed Spinach

Serves 4

The hint of nutmeg adds a perfect accent to this creamy, rich dish.

2 tbsp. butter
2 tbsp. flour
⅓ cup milk
⅓ cup chicken stock
¼ cup heavy cream
2 lb. fresh spinach, coarsely sliced
⅛ tsp. salt
Pinch of white pepper
Sprinkle of nutmeg

Make a blond roux with the butter and flour. Once flour is just cooked, whisk in milk and chicken stock. Whisk until thickened, then add heavy cream. Stir in spinach, cooking until wilted. Season with salt, white pepper, and nutmeg.

food

June 1

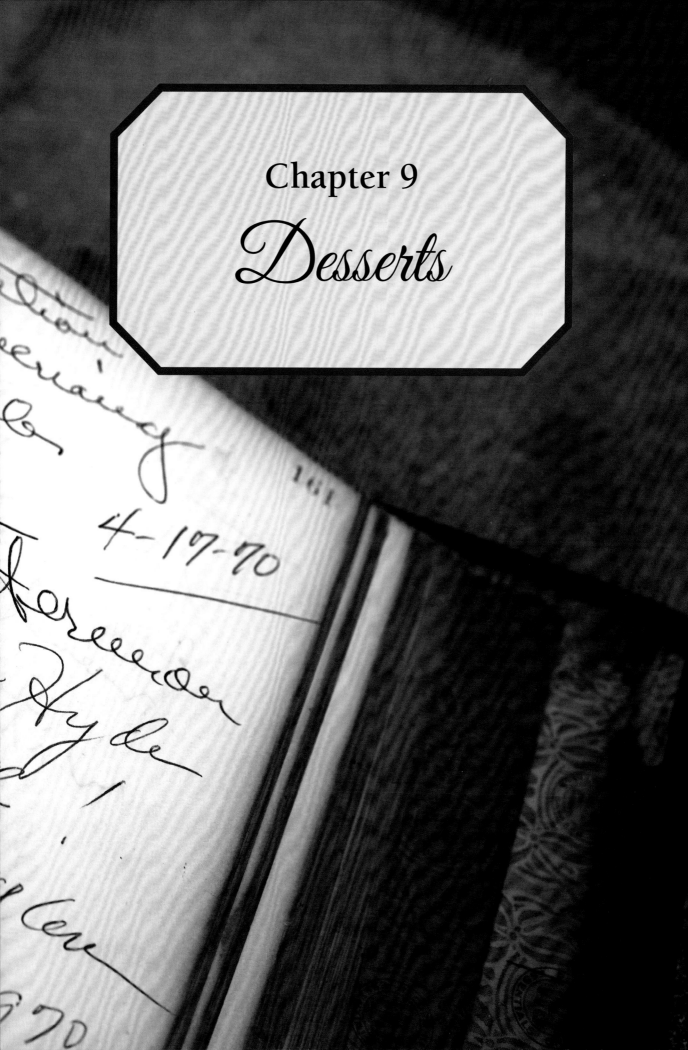

Chapter 9
Desserts

Bread Pudding with Brandy Sauce

Serves 8-10

Bread pudding is New Orleans' most ubiquitous dessert. The secret ingredient in Manale's bread pudding is a tiny bit of pineapple juice. One of fifth-generation Elizabeth DeFelice's happiest childhood memories is of standing on a chair, elbow deep in a big pan of bread pudding. Miss Bev and Karry smile fondly, remembering how she loved squeezing the milky mixture between her little fingers.

1 loaf French bread
1½ cups raisins
1 cup sugar
1 dozen eggs
6 cups whole milk
1 6-oz. can pineapple juice
1 tbsp. vanilla extract
1 cup butter, melted

Cut French bread into large squares and place in a bowl. Toss in raisins and sugar. Break eggs over bread mixture.

Add milk, pineapple juice, and vanilla extract. Mix with hands, squeezing bread mixture until all is well combined. Pour melted butter over the bread pudding and mix well.

Grease a 9x12-inch rectangular pan. Pour bread-pudding mixture into pan. Place pan in a larger rectangular pan and add water to larger pan until halfway up the side of the bread-pudding pan. Bake at 350 degrees for 1 hour and 15 minutes. Serve hot with brandy sauce.

Brandy Sauce

Yields 1½ cups

1 cup butter, softened
¼ cup brandy
½ tsp. vanilla extract
1 cup powdered sugar

Beat all ingredients together until fully blended. Serve on hot bread pudding.

(Photograph by Sam Hanna)

Pecan Pie

Serves 6-8

Miss Bev's trick of adding some reserved pecans to the pie after it begins to bake guarantees a finished pie chock full of nuts.

⅓ cup butter
⅓ cup sugar
3 eggs
½ cup Karo dark syrup
2 tsp. vanilla extract
¼ tsp. salt
1 cup pecans, chopped
1 8-inch prebaked piecrust

Preheat the oven to 350 degrees. Melt butter. Combine with sugar in a mixing bowl and cream together.

Add eggs and mix well. Add syrup, vanilla, and salt. Add ¾ cup pecans (reserving ¼ cup) and pour into piecrust.

Put pie into the preheated oven and bake for 5 minutes. With a fork, gently stir the filling in the top of pie, then sprinkle on remaining ¼ cup pecans. Continue baking for 35-40 minutes until baked through. Cool before serving.

Key Lime Pie

Serves 6-8

Before refrigeration, freestanding, insulated wooden cabinets called "iceboxes" were a fixture in every kitchen. Harvested ice from lakes and ponds in the Northeast was first shipped to New Orleans in the early 1800s but in 1868, Louisiana Ice Works on Tchoupitoulas Street became the first commercial production facility in the world to manufacture ice. The "icebox pie" is a creation that dates back to those days. With its condensed-milk filling and graham-cracker crust, Manale's Key lime pie is very similar to the classic lemon icebox pie of yesteryear.

6 egg yolks
1 8-oz. can condensed milk
6 oz. Key lime juice
1 8-inch graham-cracker piecrust

Mix together egg yolks and condensed milk with a wire whisk until smooth. Add Key lime juice. Pour into piecrust and bake for 25 minutes at 350 degrees. Cool at room temperature. Chill before serving.

Uncle Jake's Cheesecake

Serves 8-10

Mark remembers spending his early days in the restaurant, making his grandfather's favorite cheesecake first thing every morning. His uncle Jake passed the family recipe on to Mark, after making it himself for years.

Crust

5 graham crackers
¼ cup sugar
Pinch of nutmeg
Pinch of cinnamon
1 tbsp. butter, melted

Add all dry ingredients to a blender or food processor and blend to the consistency of fine crumbs. Add butter and mix thoroughly. Press mixture into the bottom of an 8-inch springform pan. Chill for 20 minutes or more.

Cake

1½ lb. Philadelphia cream cheese, softened
4 eggs
½ pint sour cream
2 oz. amaretto
1 cup sugar
½ cup half-and-half
1 tbsp. vanilla extract

Thoroughly beat together all ingredients until smooth. Pour mixture over graham-cracker crust. Place cake in a preheated 350-degree oven for 30 minutes. *Do not open the oven.* After 30 minutes, turn off the heat and allow cake to set for 45 minutes in the warm oven. Remove from oven.

Topping

½ pint sour cream
1 tsp. vanilla extract
½ tsp. lemon juice
½ can condensed milk

Heat oven to 450 degrees. Spread topping over cake and return to oven. Turn off the heat immediately and allow cake to set for 10 minutes in warm oven. Remove from oven and thoroughly chill before serving.

Uncle Jake (Photograph courtesy of Radosta Family Collection)

Chocolate Mousse

Serves 6

No matter how big the meal, there's always room for a little light-as-air chocolate mousse.

12 oz. dark chocolate chips
1 oz. brandy
1 oz. marsala
7 eggs, separated
1 cup heavy cream
2 tbsp. sugar

Melt chocolate in a double boiler. Remove from heat. Whisk brandy and marsala with egg yolks until thick and lemon colored. Slowly whisk egg-yolk mixture into the chocolate.

Whip cream to soft peaks. Whip egg whites together with sugar until soft peaks form. Fold the whipped cream into the chocolate, then fold in the egg whites. Chill for at least 1 hour.

Fill a pastry bag with mousse mixture and pipe into serving glasses. Chill again for 1 hour or more before serving. Serve topped with whipped cream if desired.

Caramel Custard

Yields 6 4-oz. servings

This classic New Orleans dessert is wickedly delicious with the Manale addition of condensed milk!

1 tbsp. water
1 cup sugar
6 eggs
1 8-oz. can condensed milk
1 can water
1 tbsp. vanilla extract
¼ tsp. salt
½ cup whipped cream

In a saucepan, combine water and sugar. Bring to a boil and watch carefully as sugar solution begins to change color. Just before it reaches a dark-brown caramel color, remove it from the heat and pour approximately 2-3 tbsp. caramel into each custard dish. Allow to cool slightly.

Beat together the eggs, condensed milk, water, vanilla, and salt. Pour into custard dishes. Place dishes in a water bath in a large baking pan. Cover with aluminum foil and bake at 350 degrees for 45 minutes, until a knife inserted into the custard comes out clean. Cool, then serve hot or chilled with whipped cream.

(Photograph by Sam Hanna)

Rachel's Tiramisu

Serves 6-8

Fifth-generation chef Rachel DeFelice first learned to love her mother's tiramisu at home. After tasting it in Italy during her culinary studies abroad, she began to tweak the original recipe to more suit her style. She makes her tiramisu in a single layer on a serving platter, but it can also be layered in a trifle bowl for an elegant presentation at the table.

½ cup heavy cream
1 tbsp. powdered sugar
¼ tsp. vanilla extract
6 large eggs, separated
2 cups plus 2 tbsp. brewed espresso or cold
   coffee concentrate, divided
1 cup sugar plus 1 tbsp. sugar, divided
¼ cup grappa or Cognac
1 1b. mascarpone cheese, chilled
24 stale ladyfingers
¼ cup unsweetened cocoa powder
Shaved semisweet chocolate

In a small mixing bowl, beat cream, powdered sugar, and vanilla until stiff peaks form. Reserve in the refrigerator for later use.

In a stainless-steel bowl, beat the egg yolks until foamy. Beat in the espresso, 1 cup sugar, and the grappa, beating continuously until thick and pale, about 1 minute. Place the bowl over a hot-water bath and continue beating for about 6-8 minutes until thickened. Once it thickens, remove from heat and beat in the cold mascarpone cheese until smooth and fully incorporated, about 3-5 minutes. Reserve in the refrigerator for later use.

In another bowl, whip the reserved egg whites until they form soft peaks. Add 1 tbsp. sugar and beat until stiff peaks form. Gently fold the whipped egg whites into the reserved mascarpone mixture.

Using a pastry brush, lightly coat 12 ladyfingers with 1 tbsp. espresso, and then line them up on the bottom of a serving dish to form the first layer. Spread half of the mascarpone mixture on top of the ladyfingers. Add a light dusting of half of the cocoa powder.

Brush the remaining 12 ladyfingers with 1 tbsp. espresso and make a second layer. Spread the remaining mascarpone mixture over the ladyfingers and dust with remaining cocoa. Spread an even layer of the reserved whipped cream on top. Garnish with shaved chocolate. Chill for at least 4 hours or overnight, in order to properly set before slicing.

(Photograph by Sam Hanna)

Italian Cream Cake

Serves 8-10

Many Italian cream cakes contain coconut, both in the cake and as a decoration, but in Louisiana, pecans are a natural, local addition. Sandy Whann, fourth generation of Leidenheimer's Baking Company, New Orleans' famous poorboy-bread bakery, remembers countless birthdays celebrated at Manale's. The reason was Manale's Italian cream cake! Although the DeFelices had lost track of the original recipe, Sandy's mom had talked them out of it years ago and luckily hung on to it so that we can all enjoy it again today.

2 cups sugar
½ cup butter, softened
½ cup vegetable oil
5 eggs
1 tsp. baking soda
1 cup buttermilk
2 cups flour, sifted
1 small can angel-flake coconut
1 cup chopped pecans
1 tbsp. vanilla extract

Cream sugar, butter, and oil until light and fluffy. Separate eggs. Add egg yolks one at a time, beating after each addition.

Add baking soda, buttermilk, flour, coconut, pecans, and vanilla. Beat well to blend. Beat egg whites until stiff and fold into batter.

Pour into 3 greased and floured 8- or 9-inch round layer-cake pans. Bake at 350 degrees for 25 minutes or so until baked through. Cool.

Frosting

8 oz. cream cheese, softened
8 oz. butter, softened
1 tsp. vanilla extract
1 lb. powdered sugar
1 cup chopped toasted pecans

Beat cream cheese and butter together. Gradually mix in vanilla and powdered sugar. Spread between cake layers and fully ice the outside of the cake. Sprinkle cake with pecans to finish.

(Photograph by Sam Hanna)

Italian Stallion

Serves 1

The Italian Stallion harks back to the 1970s, when it concluded many a meal at Manale's. When recreated by fifth-generation Thomas DeFelice, there was much amusement about a pink creamy drink with such a macho name!

1 oz. amaretto
½ oz. crème de noyaux
½ oz. white crème de cacao
3 oz. half-and-half

Combine all ingredients in a bar shaker. Fill with ice, then shake vigorously for about 1 minute. Strain liquid into a chilled, stemmed glass.

Acknowledgments

This book would not have been possible without the kind and generous cooperation and contribution of the DeFelice family. Sandy, Bob, Mark, and Ginny opened their lives and their restaurant to me. Fifth-generation Elizabeth willingly became my virtual assistant on the project. Her organization and indomitable determination were invaluable. Elizabeth's cousins, David and Rachel, provided assistance with both family lore and the fine points of several family recipes.

It was a great blessing to learn about Pascal firsthand from his nephew, Martin H. Radosta. At the time the book was written, Martin was the oldest living family member. Martin passed away surrounded by family on May 9, 2018. His long view on Manale's of the fifties, sixties, and seventies helped paint an authentic picture of the restaurant in those days. Martin's daughter, Lisa Haller, generously gave of her time and boundless knowledge of family history.

Beverly Simon, Karry Byrd, Thomas Stewart, and Darryl Keasley patiently demonstrated dishes and walked me through the preparation of Manale's classics. Chef Mark DeFelice and his daughter Rachel recreated historic dishes no longer on the menu, making it possible to bring them to life again.

My photographer, Sam Hanna, was a joy and inspiration to work with, as always. My research assistant, Katherine Edwards, added rich details to the background stories of the founder and earlier generations. Frank Maselli and Megan Celona of the American Italian Cultural Center provided important information on the lives of New Orleans' Italian immigrants. Reggie Morris's technical assistance was invaluable.

Many thanks to all.

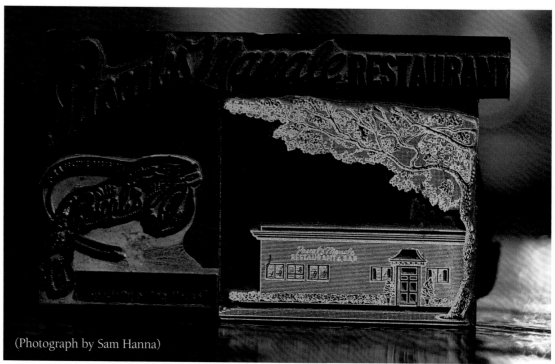

(Photograph by Sam Hanna)

222

Index

Alfredo Sauce, 120

Baked Italian Crawfish, 158
Baked Lasagna, 199
Balsamic Vinaigrette, 125
Barbeque Shrimp Poorboy, 133
Barbeque Shrimp Sauce, 111
Blue Cheese Dressing, 128
Bonano, Johnny, 46, 55
Brabant Potatoes, 203
Bread Pudding with Brandy Sauce, 210
Brisket Marinara, 172
Byrd, Karry, 46, 50, 135, 210

Calamari, 87
Caramel Custard, 215
Cavatelli Chicken Eggplant Francesca, 200
Cheese Tortellini Soup, 101
Chicken Alfredo, 181
Chicken and Broccoli Soup, 102
Chicken and Crab Napoleon, 180
Chicken Andouille Gumbo, 94
Chicken Bordelaise, 184
Chicken Cacciatore, 183
Chocolate Mousse, 214
Cocktail Sauce, 121
Combination Pan Roast, 85
Crab and Cauliflower au Gratin, 154
Crab and Corn Bisque, 99
Crab Cakes, 84
Crabmeat Ravigote, 83
Crabmeat Verdi, 155
Crawfish and Andouille Pasta, 158
Crawfish Bisque, 96
Crawfish Etouffee, 156
Creamed Spinach, 207
Creamy Italian House Dressing, 126
Creamy Manale's Grits, 205
Creole Sauce, 116

Daniels, Catherine, 43, 159
D'Antoni Sandwich, 135
Daube, 171
DeFelice, Dana, 51
DeFelice, David, 51, 82
DeFelice, Elizabeth, 51, 210

DeFelice, Esteff, 36, 51
DeFelice, Esteff, Jr., 51
DeFelice, Frances Radosta, 22, 25, 31, 37-39, 42, 50,
    140, 155, 177
DeFelice, Ginny, 39, 51
DeFelice, Marci, 51
DeFelice, Mark, 38, 42, 46, 51, 55, 122, 131, 139, 141,
    149, 174, 213
DeFelice, Rachel, 51, 174, 201, 216
DeFelice, Savare, 37-39, 42-43, 51, 107, 142
DeFelice, Savare (Sandy), Jr., 37, 42, 51
DeFelice, Savare (Tré), III, 43, 51
DeFelice, Stephen, 37-38, 42
DeFelice, Thomas, 51, 221
DeFelice, Virginia Radosta, 22, 25, 31, 37-39, 42-43,
    51, 127
Demi-Glace, 120
Dirty Rice, 202

Eggplant Dryades, 80
Eggplant Marinara, 89

Fried Oyster Spinach Salad with Warm Blue Cheese
    Dressing, 69
Frutti di Mare, 150

Garlic Mashed Potatoes, 204
Grilled Fish Orleans, 161
Gruntz, Wendy, 43, 46

Hebert, F. Edward, 22, 25
Herman, Pete, 22
Honey Mustard Dressing, 131

Insalata Manale, 129
Italian Cream Cake, 219
Italian Olive Salad, 130
Italian Stallion, 221

Keasley, Darrell, 95
Key Lime Pie, 212

Liver and Onions, 187
Locicero, Nick, 46, 55

Manale, Alice Hager, 17, 19

Manale Béarnaise Sauce, 117
Manale, Francesca, 15
Manale, Francesco, 15
Manale, Frank, 15, 17, 19-20, 135
Manale Hollandaise Sauce, 119
Manale, Mamie, 15
Manale's Meatballs, 170
Manale's Seasoned Breadcrumbs, 132
Marinara Sauce, 113
Marinated Crab Claws, 82
Mark's Barbeque Shrimp, 139
Mignonette Sauce, 124

Ossobuco, 173
Oyster and Artichoke Soup, 67
Oysters and Andouille, 73
Oysters and Spaghetti, 77
Oysters Bienville, 60
Oysters Dante, 74
Oysters En Brochette Manale Style, 69
Oysters Francesca, 71
Oyster Soup, 65
Oysters Pesto, 72
Oysters Rockefeller, 63
Oyster Stew, 64

Pan-Seared Catfish, 162
Pascal's House Dressing, 127
Pascal's Salad, 127
Pascal's Spicy Mayonnaise, 122
Pecan Pie, 211
Peteburger, 135
Poisson Catherine, 159
Portobello Pizza, 82
Prosciutto, Peppers, and Shrimp with Bowtie Pasta, 195

Rachel's Risotto, 201
Rachel's Tiramisu, 216
Radosta, Francesca Manale, 71
Radosta, Frances Sansone, 22, 28, 31
Radosta, Frank, 15, 19-20, 26
Radosta, Ginny, 42
Radosta, Jake, 15, 20, 28, 31, 37, 46, 96, 122, 213
Radosta, Lulu, 15, 22
Radosta, Mamie, 15, 22
Radosta, Martin H., 17, 26, 28, 39, 42, 170
Radosta, Martin John, 22, 25, 28, 37, 39
Radosta, Matteo (Martin) Joseph, 15, 26
Radosta, Pascal, 15, 17, 20, 22, 25-26, 28, 31, 36-37, 43, 46, 111, 122, 139, 170
Radosta, Pascal, Jr., 22, 28, 37, 39

Radosta, Peter, 15, 20, 37, 43, 135
Radosta, Vitda, 15, 22
Red Beans, 186
Red Gravy, 114
Remoulade Sauce, 123
Robinson, Frank, 50, 101
Rosemary Chicken, 185

Sansone, Johnny, 46
Sautéed Spinach, 206
Savare's Leek and Potato Soup, 107
Seafood Gumbo, 92
Shrimp a la Scarpia, 140
Shrimp and Grits, 141
Shrimp and Penne Pasta, 194
Shrimp Bisque, 98
Shrimp Creole, 145
Shrimp Diavolo, 146
Shrimp Mediterranean, 149
Shrimp Savare, 142
Shrimp Tre Formaggi, 141
Simon, Beverly, 46, 51, 131, 210-11
Softshell Crab Pascal, 166
Spaghetti Bordelaise, 193
Spaghetti Collins, 192
Split Pea Soup, 103
Stewart, Thomas, 46, 55, 107
Stuffed Artichokes, 86
Stuffed Crab, 166
Stuffed Eggplant, 153
Stuffed Mushrooms, 81
Stuffed Shrimp, 165
Stuffed Tufoli, 196
Sutro, Vincent, 31
Sweet Potato and Andouille Soup, 95

Tartar Sauce, 124
Turtle Soup, 100

Uncle Jake's Cheesecake, 213

Veal Bracioloni, 175
Veal Chop with Portobello Mushroom Demi-Glace, 174
Veal Marsala, 176
Veal Piccata, 178
Veal Puccini, 177
Vegetable Beef Soup, 104